hellenic cl

the ordering of form in the a

• • • ellipsis

• • • **a history of architecture** christopher tadgell **2**

hellenic classicism

the ordering of form in the ancient greek world

First published 1998 by
●●●ellipsis
55 Charlotte Road
London
EC2A 3QT
EMAIL ...@ellipsis.co.uk

ISBN 1 899858 39 3

Publisher Tom Neville
Designed by Jonathan Moberly
Edited by Vicky Wilson
Drawings by John Hewitt
Drawings on pages 92 and 94 generated by Matthew Taylor from a CAD model by Andrew Pollendine at Kent Institute of Art and Design
Image processing by Heike Löwenstein
Glossary by Andrew Wyllie
Index by Diana LeCore
Printed and bound in Hong Kong

British Library Cataloguing in Publication Data: a catalogue record for this publication is available from the British Library

contents

the establishment of hellas

In the second half of the second millennium BC tribes from the Aryan linguistic group of peoples – generally known as Achaeans – poured into Greece in several waves, pushing their predecessors on the mainland down the Attic peninsula and out to the islands of the Aegean Sea and the neighbouring coast of Aeolia and Ionia (modern Turkey). Related though they were, the two main branches of the Hellenes (as the Achaeans were to be called after they had settled) were to be differentiated as Ionians and Dorians. Likewise, the two main strands of classical art, woven in Ionia on the one hand and in the mainland of Greece and on the Peloponnesian peninsula on the other, were to be called Ionic and Doric.

The area into which the Achaeans penetrated had long been dominated by Crete and – through the intermediacy of the great trading power of Phoenicia with its coastal ports in modern Lebanon and Syria – by ideas from Mesopotamia. The invaders were nomadic herdsmen, their primary concern the

1 **Zeus (or Poseidon), bronze statue** c. 560 BC.
The statue was found in a shipwreck off Cape Artemision (Athens, National Museum).

appeasement of the gods of the sky, who represented the forces of nature, which they personified as male.[1] The native agriculturalists, by contrast, were primarily devoted to the mother goddess in gratitude for the mysteries of fertility and growth.[2] Fundamentally different attitudes were promoted by these two sets of concerns: the need for constant alertness and rigour in the quest for the key to placating the sky gods encouraged questioning and rationalism; devotion to the mother goddess, mysterious but secure, encouraged resignation and gratitude, sensuality and emotionalism.

Longer settled in the realm of the mother goddess, and exposed especially in their new home to her cult of the moon, the Ionians allowed their rationalist ideals to be compromised by the softer attitudes of the indigenes – no doubt often through marriage. The Dorians, on the other hand – last to relinquish a nomadic existence – stuck to an uncompromisingly

2 **Artemis of Ephesus, marble statue incorporating the fertility attributes of the Anatolian mother goddess Cybele** AD 2nd century (Selcuk, Ephesus Museum).

rationalist conception of the gods and their creation. Both saw the gods in human form – that is, as anthropomorphic – and devoted themselves to the perfection of the human image to represent them. The Dorians were obsessed with the male body; the Ionians were concerned with representing the female form, in a synthesis of Achaean ideals and those long predominant in the area.

The poems attributed to Homer and Hesiod, set down at the earliest in the first part of the 7th century BC, relate an ancient tradition of which the humanisation of the gods is the most salient feature. The inhabitants of Olympus, representing the forces of nature, are conceived in human form but have superhuman attributes which account for the extraordinary in human experience; their manoeuvres are explained in terms that represent ideals of all the traits of humanity. Hence arose myths as many and various as the Hellenic communities which emerged from the Dark Ages following the last wave of Aryan invasion. These myths defined man's relationship to the divine, exorcised his phobias about the forces of nature, and contained the impact of one way of life upon another.

The Olympian gods

The chief deity of the Achaeans was the Cretan-born sky god Zeus. The sea and the realm of the dead below the earth were the domains of his brothers, Poseidon and Hades respectively. With the assertion of the ideas of the invaders over those of the natives – and of the male over the female – Zeus married the mother goddess (called Hera by the Hellenes) and transferred her responsibility for agriculture to his sister, Demeter.

Through various extra-marital liaisons, Zeus claimed paternity over other key pre-Hellenic deities, notably the ambivalent twins Apollo and Artemis, Athena, Aphrodite and Dionysius. Apollo was the sun god, cousin of the Indo-Aryan Surya and rather more like the Assyrian Shamash than the Egyptian Re. As the propagator of plants and patron of healing and art, his mystery cult invoked the great oracles of Delphi[3] and Delos and spanned Hellas. His sister Artemis was the moon goddess, mistress of animals and patroness

3 OVERLEAF **Delphi, sanctuary of Apollo** founded early in the 6th century BC, view showing principal cult temple (in the foreground) and tholos (in the middle distance).

of the hunt, whose cult as a protectress of motherhood in Ionia assimilated the Anatolian mother goddess Cybele. Athena, patroness of ploughing, was a war goddess, like the Babylonian Ishtar, but was concerned with upholding order and promoting wise counsel in the settlement of disputes. She fought off Poseidon's challenge for Attica. Aphrodite was a goddess of procreativity, also like Ishtar, ultimately associated with love. Dionysius, like the Egyptian Osiris, was the vegetation god who dies in winter and is reborn in spring, associated with the vine and wine, intoxication, irresponsibility, ecstasy, inspiration – and theatre.

Presiding like a great king over his family court on Olympus,[4] Zeus was not omnipotent. The most primitive of natural forces were beyond his control: essentially female, but alienated from the earth mother when her realm was ceded to Hades, these sprang from depths unfathomable to reason. Their exorcism in the ritual breaching of taboo achieved state sponsorship in the fertility-mystery cults centred on Demeter and Dionysius. Represented most terrifyingly as the Furies pursuing Fate, they were recognised even by philosophers as irrational 'necessity'.

The male and female principles of the herdsmen and

4 **Olympia, Temple of Zeus** reconstructed section showing the colossal statue of Zeus enthroned.

Probably executed in the third quarter of the 5th century BC, the statue of Zeus – in ivory and gold over timber and clay (chryselephantine) – was acknowledged as the culmination of the work of Phidias and was one of the seven wonders of the world.

agriculturalists governed early architecture. The works of an earth-mother-worshipping people, baffled by the mystery of life and growth, and of sky-god worshippers, who sought the key to understanding divine purpose in the analysis of the structure of the universe, are nowhere more sharply contrasted than at Knossos and Mycenae or Tiryns (see volume I, ORIGINS, pages 175–208). The way of the invaders was now to be imposed throughout the Aegean and beyond.

Early temples

Many peoples saw their gods in the image of their king: the king was the greatest figure they knew, and

5 **The primitive house as the house of god: terracotta model from the sanctuary of Hera at Argos** late 8th century BC.

This may be a house or a temple – in either case, it is from such buildings that the process of the evolution of the temple took its departure. Remains of prehistoric temples representing various stages in the development of the house – from the circular hut through horseshoe, apsidal and rectangular forms – have been found in mainland Greece and the Aegean islands. Rarely as well built as the

Mycenaean megaron, their walls were not thick enough to carry flat roofs: the model here represents the age-old structure of wattle and daub covered with a pitched roof of mud and thatch. As tiles were adopted instead of thatch, the pitch was lowered to approximate to the shallow triangle of the later pediment.

6 **Delphi, sanctuary of Apollo, Treasury of the Athenians** c. 507 BC.

In addition to temples, many Hellenic states erected treasuries at the major sanctuaries to hold precious objects dedicated by their citizens and the regalia to be worn in cult ceremonies by their representatives. Consisting simply of the cella and portico of the primitive temple, their small scale admitted rich materials and lavish embellishment.

the gods, as super-kings, would often be worshipped in accordance with formulas derived from attendance upon the terrestrial ruler. As the settled Hellenes evolved their concept of the deity, a house was needed to supplement the primitive open-air altar favoured previously by the Achaeans (as in the main court at Tiryns, see volume 1, ORIGINS, page 204). So the megaron of the Achaean king was adopted as the form for the temple and for the small buildings erected at sanctuaries by various states as treasuries for their offerings to the gods.[6] Both megaron and temple descend from a common domestic prototype[5] which continued to dominate the rare palaces of the post-Achaean Greek world.[7]

The remains of prehistoric megarons at Thermum[8] include several with a curved room at the end – perhaps for the image of a deity. In the development of the temple, as with the megaron, greater width required the introduction of posts to provide intermediate support for the roof structure. These were placed in an extended row rather than in pairs like those framing the secular hearth. Sometimes walls closed both ends except for a door in the entrance front. Sometimes the central row of posts continued through the portico

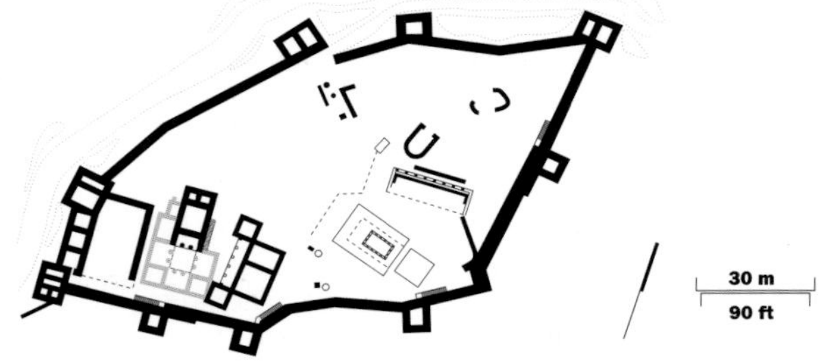

7 **Larissa, palace** 6th and early 5th century BC, plan.
The original structures, built by a vassal of the Persians, included the twin-towered pavilion with portico (1), closely following the Syrian bit-hilani prototype but clearly incorporating two megarons, and the main megaron itself (2), which was augmented c. 450 BC by a court flanked by three porticos (3), each with a pair of columns between projecting walls (distyle in antis). The introduction of the bit-hilani may have followed the precedent set by the palace of the Persian satrap at Sardis which, in turn, was probably modelled on the camp-palace of Cyrus the Great at Pasargadae (see volume 1, ORIGINS, page 217).

8 **Thermum (Aetolia)** plan of site showing late 8th-century BC apsidal and rectangular megarons (1 and 2) and the mid 7th-century BC Temple of Apollo (3).

The unique curve of posts around the megaron under the temple was possibly original. The temple, with cella and false porch (opisthodomos), had five posts at each end and 15 at the sides on a stylobate 12 by 38 metres (40 by 125 feet). The roof, originally gabled at the front end and hipped at the back, is the earliest known to have been covered with terracotta tiles. Its exposed timbers were protected by decorated panels, also of terracotta. The original timber posts had to be replaced with stone columns, and pediments were added.

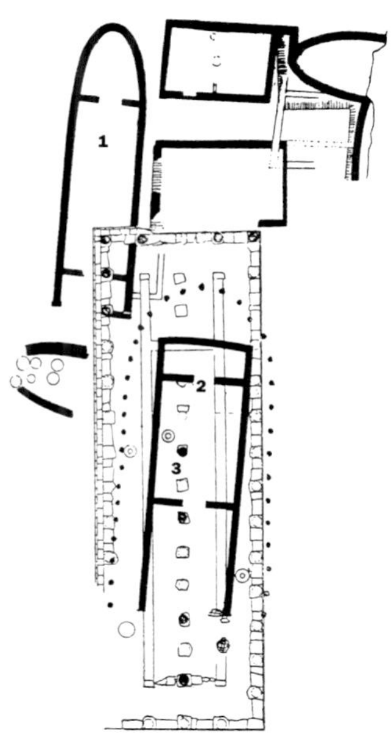

and, for perhaps the first time at Thermum, a false porch (opisthodomos) was added for symmetry at the other end. The outer columns of the central row are seen in antis (that is, between the projecting ends of the walls). Finally stone replaced timber, not only for greater durability but perhaps primarily to support the greater weight of the roofs when terracotta tiles replaced thatch or shingles – as at Thermum in the mid 7th century BC. With tile too came the lowering of the roof ridge and a strictly rectilinear plan.

At Thermum and Samos – one of the islands near the coast of Turkey which was a cult centre of Hera[9] – we can trace the evolution of the temple from a walled structure with central columns to a structure

9 **Samos, Heraeum (Temple of Hera)** reconstructed plans as founded in the first quarter of the 8th century BC and as rebuilt c. 675 BC.

Soon after its construction the original temple building was given a protective verandah (pteron). The earliest yet known, it remained rare for at least a century. The cella, originally 6.5 by 32.9 metres (21 feet 4 inches by 108 feet), was widened to 6.8 metres (22 feet 4 inches). The addition of the pteron originally took the overall dimensions to 9.5

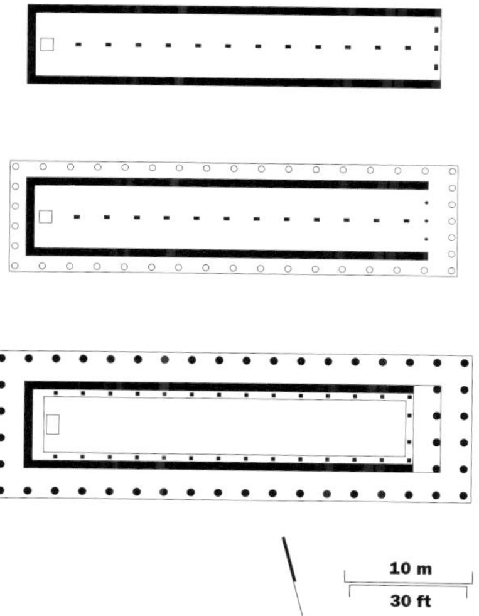

by 36.9 metres (31 by 121 feet) and widening to 11.7 metres (38 feet) produced 3.2:1 as the ratio of length to width. The displacement of the intermediate supports from the centre to the sides produced six-post (hexastyle) porticos and left the cult image unobstructed within.

surrounded by a verandah (pteron) to protect the mud-brick walls from the forces of the elements. To leave a clear space in which the image of the deity would not be obscured, the central supports of the Heraeum (Temple of Hera) at Samos were replaced by parallel rows of posts tied to those of the pteron. The temple faced an uncovered altar, as did the king's megaron at Tiryns, aligned towards the rising sun – as was to become the norm. Before following the evolution of the classical Hellenic temple from these primitive beginnings, let us look at the development of the society responsible for it.

The Aegean was a cradle of civilisation, but unlike Egypt and Mesopotamia, where irrigation from the grand river systems made lucrative crop farming on a large scale practicable, its agriculture was confined to narrow valleys or strips of alluvial plain separated by rugged and often well-forested mountains. The Hellenic corps which took these valleys settled about some defensible eminence (acropolis) from which they managed the land. Each settlement (polis) was to preserve such distinction as topography and geography provided, despite a general sense of linguistic affinity in the face of unintelligible 'barbarians'.

Self-sufficiency was a sustainable ideal among frugal people who could live much of life outdoors. Their polity was moulded accordingly. With open access to the sea, prosperity was furthered through combining agriculture with fishing, trade and mercenary soldiering abroad. Ideas came with cargo along the sea lanes developed by the Phoenicians, of course, but the Mediterranean in general was quiet in the centuries over which the Hellenic communities were evolving and no external pressure forced interdependence on them to eclipse their individuality. On the contrary, their individual needs for more land to cope with population growth and, later, for trading posts in areas rich in grain or minerals – together with adventurous navigation – led to far-flung colonisation from the mid 8th century BC. As a result, the Greek world ultimately extended from the shores of the Black Sea to Sicily and southern Italy, southern France and Spain.

The birth of democracy

Trade led to specialisation and a market economy. This process was accelerated in areas where the soil was too poor to grow enough grain for an expanding urban population – as in Attica, where only the olive thrived and, apart from oil, pottery and silver paid for imported corn. The community of farmers became a market town and trade surpassed land as a source of wealth, though land conveyed status in the aristocratic societies which had emerged from the Dark Ages following the fall of the heroic kings described by Homer. The new affluence of the traders led to reform.

As more people could afford to arm themselves effectively, disciplined co-operation in cohesive ranks of infantry outweighed the virtuoso contribution of the mounted elite in the armed conflicts provoked by incessant rivalry between the polities. The new trading class promoted the ideal of collective action following communal discussion among all the members of a citizenry never too large for open-air assembly (except in Sparta, where the citizen minority enslaved the conquered majority with austere rigidity). Atypical in size and commercial enterprise, Athens led the way. Early in the 6th century BC her law-giver Solon limited the size of land holdings and the aristocratic monopoly on decision-making which had supplanted the monarchy in the Dark Ages. By these means Solon protected the interests of small farmers and encouraged specialised traders.

A sense of 'commonwealth' emerged from these 6th-century reforms, though not across the geographical boundaries which fragmented Hellas. In an era of dramatic change, the rule of the individual (tyranny) was to curtail freedom in several states for a generation or two, and the rule of the few (oligarchy) sometimes did so later. But the rule of the many (democracy) was the evolving ideal – often under the direction of responsible oligarchs or even monarchs. Athens, for instance, prospered under the tyranny of Peisistratos (561–527 BC), but rejected his somewhat less enlightened sons in 510 BC. Going on to abolish clan grouping and property qualification for the election of the principal officers of state, Athens entered the classical age of the 5th century BC with a political organism of unprecedented representativeness – restriction of citizenship to native kinsmen and the existence of slavery notwithstanding.

The polis

The classical polis (inadequately translated as 'city-state' since it transcended the urban and, indeed, the territorial) was dependent on the assembly of all its citizens for the determination of policy and the administration of justice. But it was no mere association for security or economy: it was a focus for all the aspirations of morality, sensibility and intellect, secular and religious indivisibly; it was a community of shared ideals imparted in school and gymnasium and expressed in the games or festival arena and theatre as essentially as in the legislative assembly or before the temple; it was a living organism to every aspect of whose being every citizen contributed directly through his membership of a multiplicity of social groups.

Ideally of no more than 10,000 citizens, the polis overcame individualism by binding the citizen into an intricate web of associations. But its autonomy under its patron deity (invariably one of the Olympians worshipped by all Hellenes) was never overridden by a Hellenic community of culture. Beyond language, it was his sense of the dignity of man, of his freedom, which set the Greek apart from the barbarian: he was a citizen, not a subject; his government was responsible, not arbitrary. And this unique democracy depended on the scale of the polis.

The league of states

The age of the classical polis opened with the frustration of the attempts of the Persians to absorb the European mainland of Hellas into their empire, as they had absorbed Ionia. Disunited and always subject to eastern influences transmitted through the Anatolian hinterland, the Achaean settlements in Ionia were brought under the hegemony of Lydia in c. 570 BC by King Croesus, who ruled from Sardis until he in turn fell to Cyrus the Great in 546 BC. The Persian invasions of Greece in the first two decades of the 5th century BC, launched by Darius I and furthered by Xerxes I partly to secure Ionia, were defeated largely at the hands of Sparta and Athens.

The confidence with which the Athenians in particular emerged from the initial disaster of destruction by the invaders took them to unprecedented achievement. But at the head of a league dedicated to freeing their relatives in Ionia from the Persians – and to guaranteeing the maritime commerce on which their increasingly specialised economy depended – the Athenians were overweening. They enforced subscription, prevented secession and diverted league funds to Athenian purposes, in particular the rebuilding of the Acropolis devastated by the Persians (see pages 115–57). Wary that an institution for countering imperialism was becoming an instrument for its furtherance, many of the other states turned to the championship of jealous Sparta. Though rising to one of the highest points in the history of civilisation, Hellas fell to exceptionally sordid economic and political wrangling in the second half of the 5th century BC – and ultimately to the Peloponnesian War.

Philosophy

Since morality was the concern of society, unprecedented philosophical enquiry into the rights and obligations of the individual was both cause and effect of the development of the polis. And such enquiry extended to the order of the gods.

A millennium after it was woven in the Dark Ages, the mythology of invasion was embroidered by Greek and Roman poets into the chronicles of libidinous frivolity which deny decorum to Zeus' court on Olympus. Morality was not the original purpose of the gods, but even in Homer there is a dim recognition that, like humanity, the gods are subject to the principles of a grand design – to Fate or Law – and, unlike humanity, they can see the logic of the whole. Popularly credited to Zeus, Lord of Oaths, Law was Order, and if the order of the universe was not apparent to senses attuned to the experience of this world, its logic could be grasped by Reason. Most approached the divine in the traditional way, without necessarily taking the myths literally, but at the highest intellectual level myth was supplanted by philosophy, by enquiry into the nature of Order without any necessary denial of divinity. As nature and human nature were not distinguished, that Order was seen as moral as well as material.

Denying the evidence of their senses – ultimately maintaining the relevance only of Reason in seeking after Truth – the first philosophers postulated unity beyond diversity, variously reducing all the material of creation to a single element, or the nature of reality to a single condition. First seen as water – doubtless not without reference to the creation myths of the great river valleys – and subsequently as unknowable to the senses, this element was later defined as Mind itself (which might even be called Zeus). Two of the most influential early philosophers, Heracleitus and Parmenides, saw the nature of reality respectively as constant flux and the immutable homogeneity of existence behind apparent change. The Eclectics selected and recombined all they thought best from this and more.

Mathematics and music

With the revelation of the inner logic of mathematics, the definitive element was seen to be Number. The geometry of natural phenomena was persuasive, but Pythagoras of Samos was seduced by the mathematical basis of musical harmony – the realisation that musical intervals may be expressed as mathematical ratios. About 530 BC he emigrated to southern Italy, where he was strongly influenced by the reformed

Dionysian mystery cult inspired by the divine musician Orpheus, who had entered and left the world of the dead. Orphics believed that man has a divine soul condemned to endless reincarnation by the polluting matter of the body. Seeking the permanent release of the individual soul to union with World Soul, they substituted ascetic abstraction for the physical intoxication which gave temporary release to the Dionysiac. Out of their abstraction they transmitted a magic formula revealed by Orpheus as a guide to the passage.

To Pythagoras, at least, that formula was mathematical and the soul's release was the knowledge of Truth: harmony, the music of the spheres which resolves itself into Number, above all into the 1 of eternal Reality beyond this illusory world, the supreme Good, God. God's creation is all Number, the linear and volumetric manifestation of which is the geometry of its molecular elements. Thus, generated by pure thought from the objective Truth, Pythagorean geometry was theological, and the key to the transcendent beyond the subjective experience of observation, Pythagorean Rationalism was mystical. Imbibed by Plato, this potent mixture was to have a profound effect on the development of European thought.

10 **Apollo: the power of music** painted kylix, early 5th century BC (Delphi, Archaeological Museum).

Awe for the forces of nature was always to sustain an irrational strain in popular Greek religion. However, the essentially social attempt to fathom the universe as a rational creation – which advanced logic, mathematics and geometry as branches of theology – also moulded the production of houses and images for the Olympians as ideal personifications of those forces. The temple and the image of the deity – or the devotee – were the main subjects of classical art. In the constant quest for perfection, the subjection of structure to an intellectual concept founded on the timeless symmetry of mathematics clearly differentiates it from all that went before, no matter how important much of that was as inspiration. At the moment of triumph, however, Aryan reason alone was found wanting: vitality was generated only in cross-fertilising it with Aegean irrationality.

The idea of order

Hand in hand with the transition of structure from timber to stone went the evolution of the idea of architectural order. The temple was to house the god, and the god's house had to reflect the work of the gods in ordering creation: it had to represent the perfection of their order. The principles underlying that order in its totality – the macrocosm – could be deduced from the study of man, the microcosm created by the gods after their own image. Since divine perfection was inconceivable in the diversity of human identities, the object of that study was ideal: the image of man as god.

The anthropomorphic ideal

Dedicated to the representation of an anthropomorphic ideal, Hellenic art is called classical precisely because it depends upon the classification of a range of observations to determine the mean between the extremes – a rational process of comparison, selection and synthesis. Take a sample of athletes, let us say, average the measurements of all the parts of their bodies to establish means, abstract those which come closest to the mean, and recombine them to produce the idealised form. The ideal evolved with increasing rigour, and the substitution of marble for stone, admitting unprecedented precision, was the key to the perfection of the process. Structural logic is the essence of classical art, yet the Hellenic artist came to see that intellectual abstraction led to aridity and that vitality sprang from physical sensation.

The period before the classical mean was defined in the second half of the 5th century BC is known as archaic; the archaic kouros[11] and kore[12] represent the foundations upon which the anthropomorphic ideal was to be realised by the Dorians and Ionians respectively. Stripped to the bare essentials, the male kouros figure is certainly not natural: the rationalist approach to the conception of its design is governed by a mechanical sense of symmetry and exaggerated geometry in the differentiation of the parts. The Ionian conception of female form is much less rigid. Cohabiting with Aegean mother-goddess worshippers and familiar in their adopted homeland with attitudes and motifs carried across the sea from Egypt and Mesopotamia by the Phoenicians or brought home by mercenaries from the service of Assyrian kings, the earlier Achaean settlers in Ionia tempered their native rationalism with a certain sensuality. Their kore is rationalist in her proportions but also appeals to the senses through the ephemeral beauty of her costume and the styling of her hair.

Seeking the ideal synthesis in the image of humanity, the Greeks were doing two things with the house in which that ideal image was to be placed: they were

11 **Kouros**
possibly Boeotian
marble, c. 560 BC
(London, British
Museum).

12 **Kore**
Attic marble,
c. 510 BC (Athens,
Acropolis Museum).

making its structure durable and secure by replacing timber with stone, and at the same time were refining its proportions in line with their conception of ideal human form. The Doric and Ionic systems – evolved simultaneously from the male and female ideal respectively – are called the Orders because they enshrine the principles for ordering design. Beyond the conventional arrangement of the parts, the set of mathematical proportions underlying each is the key to the coherence of building design – it orders building and introduces a sense of integrity because these mathematical principles inform all the parts of the work.

The Doric Order

Presumably derived from the structure of primitive temples like those at Thermum (see 8, page 21) and Samos (see 9, page 23), the Doric Order was wholly pragmatic in origin – that is, its conventions were drawn from the practical necessities of a timber trabeated structural system.[13] When translated into stone,[14] all the parts were represented, but their natural slender proportions were lost to inefficiency in the handling of the heavy new material. Not valued aesthetically by

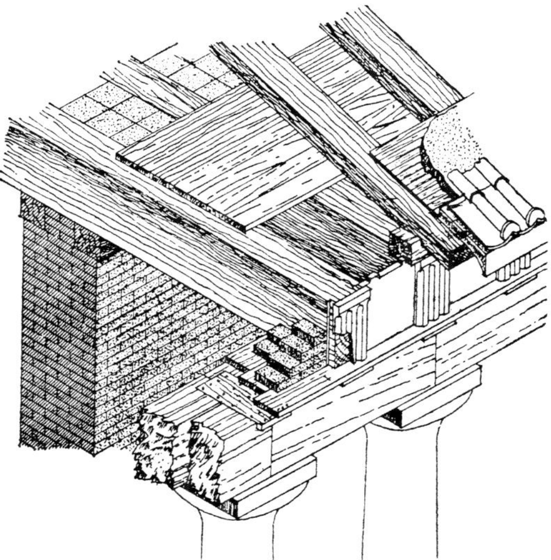

13 **The Doric Order, primitive timber structure** conjectural restoration (after Dinsmoor, though not uncontroversial).

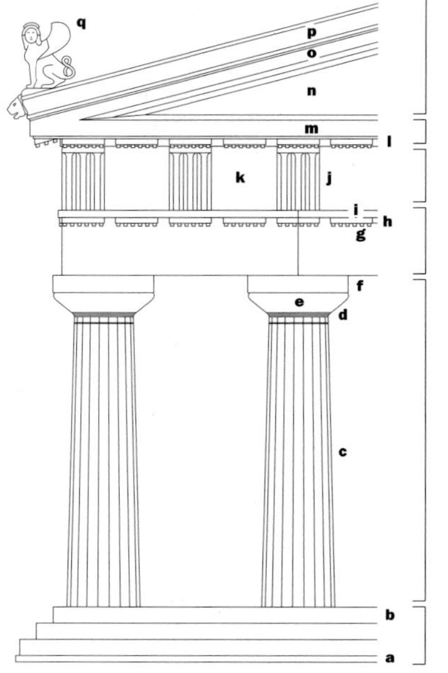
q
p
o
n
m
l
k
j
i
h
g
f
e
d
c
b
a
6
5
4
3
2
1

14 **The mature Doric Order of stone.**

Crepidoma (1) of euthynteria (a) and stylobate (b); column (2) with shaft (c) and capital of trachelion (d), echinus (e) and abacus (f); entablature of architrave (3), frieze (4) and cornice (5) with guttae (g), regula (h), tenia (i), triglyph (j), metope (k), mutule (l) and corona (m); pediment (6) with tympanum (n), raking corona (o), sima (p) and acroterium (q).

Columns were sometimes monolithic, but were usually composed of drums turned on a lathe and joined by dowels of wood or metal. The shafts were fluted in situ, usually with 20 concave grooves recalling the impressions of a curved adze in the dressing of tree trunks. The top of the shaft and the capital were usually of a single block, but the junction was bevelled. The trachelion grooves, recalling the binding to prevent timber posts from splitting, were incised with increasing emphasis for clear definition. The shaft was tapered from bottom to top, in reverse of Cretan practice (see volume 1, ORIGINS, page 186). This was decreased gradually, and in conformity with the widening of the upper diameter the slope of the echinus was reduced progressively to effect a tauter relationship between load and support. Pursuing efficiency in the use of stone, temple-builders took the proportions of the column beyond the apparent perfection achieved in the mid 5th century BC to ever more slenderness, and decreased the weight of the entablature.

As architrave and beam were doubtless of the same width in timber, they could be superimposed in the same plane over the centres of the corner columns. After the introduction of heavy roof tiles, however, the architrave needed to be stouter than the beams resting on it, especially over intercolumniations. So if the outer faces of the beam and architrave were to be kept in the same plane, the beam had to be displaced from the centre of the corner columns. To allow for the equal spacing of the beams and mutules along the sides, the width of the metopes was adjusted and the space between the last two columns of each side (that is, the intercolumniation next to each corner) was diminished after the precedent probably set by the Heraeum at Olympia (see 26, page 69).

Because of its colour and ease of handling, terracotta continued to play an important part in the decoration of the temple long after the transition from timber to masonry. But well before the end of the 6th century BC it had usually been supplanted by stone carving in various degrees of relief, and paint. Metope carvings were always in partial relief but pedimental sculpture appears the Hellenes, incidentally, the arch was relegated to hidden utility.

The column and the architrave are obviously the post and beam. Between them, the main capital motifs (echinus and abacus, recalling Cretan and Mycenean forms) express the need to cushion the impact of load on support, to protect the post from splitting. The incised rings at the top of the shaft retain the impression of binding for further reinforcement. The joists carried by the beams had exposed ends cut across the grain in timber, which needed protection: this was evidently provided by attaching terracotta tiles moulded so as to marry grooves cut into the timber, hence the triglyphs which distinguish the frieze of the Doric Order. The pegs which held the timbers together reap-

in the round from this time. The main cornice fascia, the architrave and the column were always left uncoloured but the rhythm of the frieze was enhanced by contrasting dark blue triglyphs, regulae and mutules with the red inherited from terracotta for the plane surface of the metopes. This was reflected on the underside of the cornice. Carved parts of the guttae or capital were highlighted in contrasting colours, and figures were often equipped with gilt bronze.

15 **Acragas (Agrigento), Sicily, Temple of Olympian Zeus, elevation details with atlantes** (as restored by Koldewey).

This gargantuan work – at nearly 53 by 110 metres (173 by 361 feet) the largest of the Doric temples – was furthered in celebration of victory over the Carthaginians in 480 BC but may well have been conceived before the end of the 6th century BC to eclipse the contemporary Temple of Apollo at Selinus.

The colossal scale dictated the pseudo-peripteral plan: seven by 14 widely spaced half-columns, nearly 4 metres (13 feet) in diameter and perhaps 20 metres (66 feet) high, were built of ashlar masonry and embedded in external walls. As the intercolumniations could not be bridged by single blocks of stone, the atlantes – accommodated in recessions to the upper walls – are most plausibly seen as providing intermediate support for the ashlar masonry of the entablature. The string course supporting these atlantes included an Ionic ovolo moulding and, like Ionic but contrary to Doric practice, the Order was given a base. Pilasters relieved the inner faces of the peripheral walls and square piers punctuated the screen walls of the cella. The latter was nearly 14 metres (46 feet) wide and the problem of roofing it may have remained unresolved.

pear in stone below the triglyphs as guttae. The joists carried the inclined rafters of a pitched roof. The acroteria covered the ends of the ridge beam and were often repeated at corners; antefixes covered the joints between the tiles; lions' heads framed drainage spouts. The ends of the rafters (mutules) and the fascia bordering the lowest row of tiles (corona) are visible in the overhanging eaves (cornice) all around hipped roofs; below the gable ends of pitched roofs (pediments) these are repeated against logic for symmetry. The voids between the joists (metopes) and that within the pediment (tympanum) were filled with relief sculpture relating self-contained episodes of mythology relevant to the dedicatee. Ornament is again disciplined by structure, as at Mycenae.

In the transition from timber to stone, elements irrelevant to the new material became decorative. This may seem illogical, but given a need for decorative relief (forthrightly to be denied early in the 20th century), surely it is more logical to find it in terms derived from building than in nature at large – to remember

16 **Acragas, Temple of Olympian Zeus, atlante** (Agrigento, Archaeological Museum).

structure in ornament and use ornament to articulate structural principles. This is what is meant by an architectonic approach to decoration and it was to be characteristic of high classicism throughout the western tradition.

The concept of order in Greek architecture derives from the relationship of the column to the human ideal. The equation was no more than qualitative so long as bulk was exaggerated for strength in the design of the column, but increasing efficiency in the use of stone meant that the column approached the canonical proportions of the mature male athlete towards the middle of the 5th century BC. Well before that, however, anthropomorphic abstraction sometimes ceded to literal manifestation, images of load-bearing men (atlantes) replacing or supplementing the column – as in the Temple of Olympian Zeus at Acragas (Agrigento) in Sicily.[15–16]

The Ionic Order

As in their sculpture (see 12, page 39), the Ionians tempered rationalism with sensuality in the evolution of their Order of architecture, representing woman in place of the column by the caryatid – as in the portico of the Siphnian Treasury at Delphi (see 21, page 57). Everything in the Doric Order may be explained in terms of structure, but this is not the case with the Ionic Order. Here, the dentils represent joists and the volutes acquired by the bracket capital towards the middle of the 6th century BC play the same cushioning role as the Doric echinus. But such considerations do not fully explain the forms of either element.

The derivation of the Ionic capital is controversial: some see rams' horns in it; others more plausibly relate it to the curled tendrils of a vine, the fronds of the Mesopotamian palmette or the petals of the Egyptian lotus (see volume I, ORIGINS, pages 46 and 62). It was anticipated by the so-called Aeolic capital,[17] which certainly derived from these sources, with an appreciation of the decorative value of stylised plant life and growth common to people mesmerised by fertility. But the Aeolians and their southern neighbours the Ionians may have drawn on these sources independently of each other: a capital with spiral volutes connected horizontally over an egg-and-dart ovolo dating from as early as 566 BC was found at the Milesian trading colony of Naucratis in Egypt.[18] Moreover, contrary to Doric and even Aeolic practice, the relatively slender

17 **Aeolic capitals** recovered from the early 6th-century BC sites at Larissa and Neandria.

The rising volutes characteristic of the Aeolic capital (but not of the Ionic) clearly recall the lotus motif of Egypt. The related Mesopotamian palmette is inserted between the volutes. The torus with leaf pattern was a base moulding in Assyria.

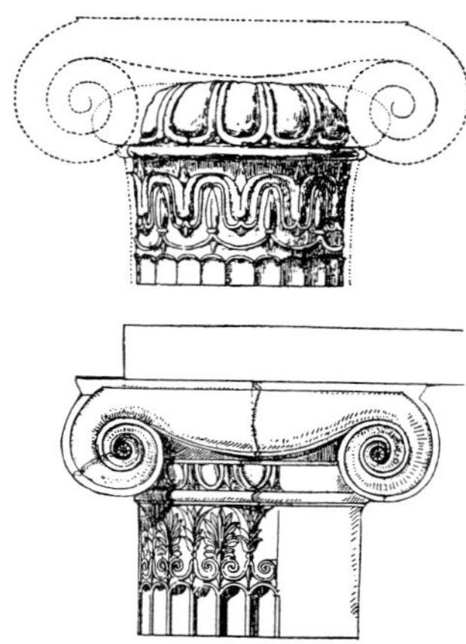

18 **Ionic capitals** from the Temple of Apollo at Naucratis (a Milesian colony in Egypt), c. 566 BC, and the Maraza Temple at Epizephyrian Locri (southern Italy), c. 450 BC.

Anticipated in the Egyptian lotus valance of the column from Naucratis, the alternating palmettes and lotuses of Locri constitute the hybrid Mesopotamian/Egyptian anthemion moulding.

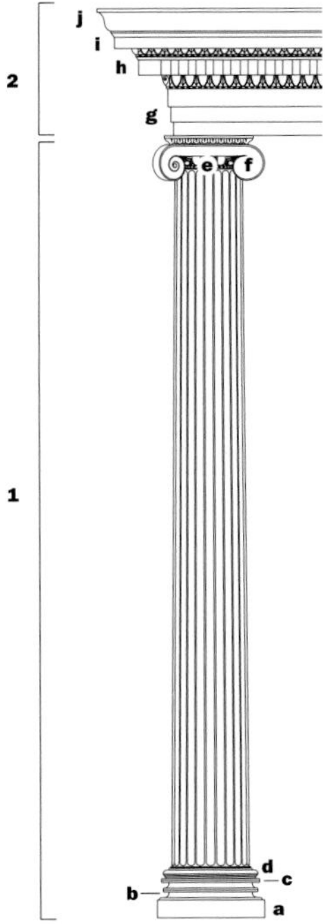

19 **The Ionic Order** from the Temple of Athena Polias at Priene, mid 4th century BC.

(1) Column and base with plinth (a), scotias (b), spira (c) and torus (d), shaft and capital with egg-and-dart moulding (e) and volutes (f); (2) entablature of architrave (g), frieze of dentils (h) and cornice of corona (i), and sima (j).

The main problem arising from the incision of the Ionic volute on the bracket of a timber structural system was how to treat the corners. If the outer face of a corner capital was parallel to the architrave of the front, as decorum dictated, it would obviously present its butt-end to the side elevation. So long

Ionic column retains a base. The torus is its most common motif, but superimposed astragal and scotia mouldings may also be included.

If the proportions of the Ionic column were lighter than those of the Doric,[19] representing the ideal maiden rather than the mature male, so too was the load it carried. But the entablature was richer in decorative mouldings. The three-tiered architrave often carries the dentils directly over an egg-and-dart ovolo, but an interpolated frieze could include a continuous figurative narrative – as in the Siphnian Treasury at Delphi[20–21] – after the example of the reliefs on the

as the length of the original bracket was emulated, two capitals were crossed with one another at right angles at the corners. With contraction in the 5th century BC, however, adjacent volutes of two perpendicular faces were bent forward to project together at the corners.

The form of base shown here was usual in Ionia. An alternative, developed in Athens, had a single scotia separating two torus mouldings, the lower one broader than the upper one. Unlike the Ionians, the Athenians preferred narrative friezes, sometimes in addition to dentils, and their architraves sometimes had only two fascias.

20 **Delphi, Siphnian Treasury, frieze** c. 530 BC (Delphi, Archaeological Museum).

The Siphnian Treasury at Delphi was built entirely of marble but conformed to the megaron prototype with cella and inset twin-columned porch (distyle in antis). It has the earliest-known Ionic entablature to incorporate a frieze embellished with figures in high relief over the plain architrave. Setting a standard to be emulated by Ionic architects, the door had a cornice supported on single-volute consoles above a triple lintel and jambs, the outer one carved with the anthemion motif.

21 **Delphi, Siphnian Treasury, caryatid** (Delphi, Archaeological Museum).

dados and parapets of Mesopotamia, or stylised floral motifs like the palmette and rosette. Continuous bands of both these types first appear in the sima as the setting for the lion-head drainage spouts. The double curve of the cyma recta here was developed from the Egyptian cavetto by curving the bottom inwards.

The rulers of Ionia loved display. Emulating the magnificence of the hypostyle halls of Egypt (see volume 1, ORIGINS, page 133), they commissioned colossal temples with two colonnades all round (dipteral) aligned with sumptuous open-air altar platforms. The fabulously wealthy King Croesus of Lydia led, with the transformation of the Heraeum at Samos and the Artemisium (Temple of Artemis) at Ephesus, c. 560 BC. The former was further developed after 530 BC on the largest scale ever attempted by the Hellenes, but never completed. The latter, destroyed by fire in 356 BC and rebuilt on the same plan, embraces the evolution of the Ionic Order from the archaic to the classical.[22]

The Artemisium had a deep porch, a cella containing the original shrine of Artemis rebuilt as a miniature temple, and a shallow opisthodomos. The columns of the double pteron were exceptionally rich: their bases established the norm of a square plinth and three superimposed pairs of astragals separated by scotias and surmounted by a torus; the lowest drum was sometimes carved with figures in low relief.[25] The densely fluted shafts, some necked with an anthemion valance, raised the capital to a height equal to some

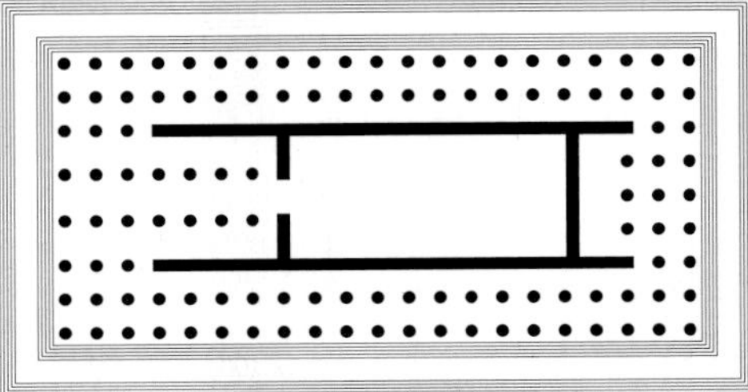

22 **Ephesus, Artemisium (Temple of Artemis)**
c. 560 BC, destroyed by fire in 356 BC, plan, and restored perspectives after 560 (RIGHT) and 356 (FAR RIGHT).

Built entirely of marble but now a mere platform supporting one column and rubble, this great work was described by several antique commentators including Vitruvius – the Roman engineer who dedicated his treatise on architecture to Octavian Caesar in 27 BC – and the encyclopaedist Pliny the Elder, who compiled his *Historia*

Naturalis early in the 2nd century AD. The ancient sources attribute the work to Theodorus of Samos and Chersiphom of Knossos, who was suceeded by his son Metagenes.

Facing west like the primitive Temple of Artemis which it enshrined, the Artemisium stood on a stylobate of two steps, c. 56 by 110 metres (c. 171 by 358 feet). This was possibly smaller than that of the contemporary Heraeum at Samos, also attributed to Theodorus of Samos, but the peristyle of the Heraeum was smaller because a wider gap was left between the edge of the platform and the bases of the columns.

The west front of the Artemisium was octastyle; the intercolumniations increased in width from the sides to the centre – where one slab spanned 8.6 metres (28 feet 3 inches) – and the columns in thickness. The east end had nine columns, the central one obviating the great span of the front and closing the axis beyond the blind wall of the opisthodomos. Each side had 21 columns, those framing the end bays set further apart than the rest to give a sense of lightness to the vast structure. In contrast to the strength of Doric reinforced by narrowing the corner bays, this has been interpreted by some as weakness. Responding to the 55 columns of the outer peristyle were 47 inner columns. There was also a third row of four columns before the pronaos. Four pairs of columns in the pronaos suggest the division of the cella into nave and aisles for the support of the roof, though as this may have been inhibited by the preservation of the original shrine within, the cella was possibly left unroofed (hypethral).

The torus of the column bases was sometimes treated to pendant foliage mouldings but usually grooved horizontally to form alternating broad and narrow convexities. This style of fluting was later adopted for Ionic shafts, but here the shafts had simple concave grooves, as with Doric. According to ancient commentators, 36 of the columns – possibly the front four rows and those of the pronaos – had drums carved with figures in low relief, and the proportions of height to base diameter were 8:1. This presumably referred to the colums of the sides and east end, which were 1.6 metres (5 feet 2 inches) in diameter at base, rather than those in the centre of the west end, which progressed to 1.9 metres (6 feet 2 inches).

After the catastrophe of 356 BC the temple was rebuilt on a higher platform – 51.4 by 111.5 metres (168 feet 8 inches by 365 feet 9 inches) by Paeonius of Ephesus and Demetrius 'the slave of Artemis'. Rising to 17.65 metres (57 feet 11 inches), the columns were higher than their predecessors, with uniform diameters of 1.84 metres (6 feet 1/2 inch), giving proportions of 9.6:1. Bases were of the usual Ionian type – with scotias and a torus – and were set on plinths (see 25, page 66). There were still 36 sculpted base drums, some by Scopas – some square (in the pronaos and opisthodomos) and some round (in the first two rows of the west end). Some of the earlier columns had 48 flutes, but the later ones seem all to have had 24. The earlier expansiveness of volute (see 23, page 64) was reduced in the mid 4th-century capitals to accord with a near-square abacus (see 24, page 65).

24 **Ephesus, Artemisium, column capital** c. 356 BC, with archaic capital in the background (London, British Museum).

23 **Delphi, Naxian column.**

The expansiveness of the volute is similar to that of the early columns of the Artemisium at Ephesus, c. 560 BC (Delphi, Archaeological Museum).

25 **Ephesus, Artemisium, column base** c. 356 BC (London, British Museum).

eight diameters after 560 BC and to more than nine after 356 BC. The early capital was elongated like a bracket and its volute spiral, masked by a rosette or entwined with an astragal, was convex in profile[23] rather than concave, as was the norm when the temple was rebuilt.[24] The triple architrave, usual in Ionia, probably derived from the original work. Dentils rested on a huge egg-and-dart ovolo in both phases. There is no trace of a narrative frieze, but the sima parapet had figures in low relief alternating with lion-head spouts.

Archaic temples of the Dorian mainland

The progeny of the Heraeum at Samos and the Artemisium at Ephesus were many in Ionia and its islands. Displaying a wide variety of stylised floral ornament with various permutations of the Order, Ionian temples were varied in plan and scale, but grandeur was the norm. The stone temples of the Dorian mainland, by contrast, were modest in scale, simple in plan and increasingly strict in regularity, as the conventions essential to the concept of order evolved. Some had only porticos, like the sanctuary treasuries which recall the primitive form (see 6, page 18), but most of the main archaic Doric temples were surrounded by a peristyle with six columns on the ends (hexastyle) and 15 or more along the sides, as in the Heraeum at Olympia.[26] The cella within, usually divided into a nave and aisles by two rows of internal columns, was preceded by a porch and backed by a matching opisthodomos, each with two columns between the projecting walls (distyle in antis).

Virtually all significant early archaic works in mainland Greece were rebuilt after the middle of the 6th century BC, apart from the Heraeum of Olympia. Reputedly originally dedicated to Zeus too, this shrine was so venerable that the replacement of its timber structure by stone seems to have been done in a piecemeal manner, as the timber rotted over the course of generations. Varied in proportion and age, the remaining columns are the most significant representatives of early archaic form. The structure clearly

26 **Olympia, Heraeum** founded late 8th century BC, plan as rebuilt early 6th century BC.

On a stylobate 18.75 by 50 metres (61 feet 6 inches by 164 feet) – a ratio of 1:2.66 – were six by 16 columns. In AD 173 the Roman commentator Pausanias recorded

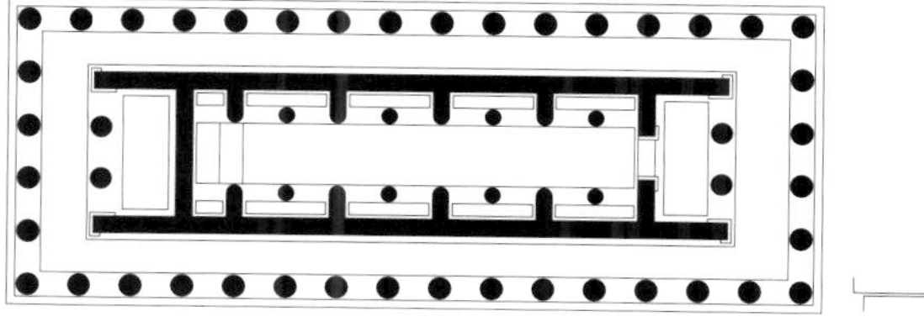

that one timber post remained in the opisthodomos; the rest were of stone. The surviving supports, a few of which are monolithic, differ considerably in diameter. The original timber posts are estimated by Dinsmoor to have been 0.98 by 5.22 metres (3 feet 2 inches by 17 feet 1 inch); the later stone columns ranged from 1 metre (3 feet 3½ inches) to 1.28 metres (4 feet 2½ inches) by 5.22 metres (17 feet 1 inch), giving proportions of between 1:5.22 and 1:4.08.

Except at the corners, where the intercolumniations were narrowed because the triglyphs were displaced to the edges, the columns of each end were slightly further apart than those along the sides since the central ones were aligned with those in antis in the porches, giving the entrance a sense of greater openness.

27 **Olympia, Heraeum** view of remains.

developed from a walled enclosure to one protected by a pteron; inside, the columns displaced from the centre were attached alternately to short spur walls at the sides. In ruins in its beautiful glade, it is easy to see the temple as a sacred grove, with posts for trees[27] – and there the origin of the garden lies.

The colonies

Doric works in the west were less rigorously logical than their mainland contemporaries. Often heterodox in form, they emulated the shrines of the Ionians in scale and embellishment. The Temple of Artemis at Corfu[28] is the pre-eminent example. With eight columns to its ends, it seems to have set a standard of opulence emulated in the colonies further west, all far richer and more ostentatious than the cities of the homeland. The Sicilians – followed by the Italians – were more interested in experiment than convention, as is demonstrated by Temple C at Selinus (Selinunte)[29] or the Temple of Olympian Zeus at Acragas (see 15, page 46), both in Sicily, and the Temple of Hera I ('Basilica') and Temple of Athena at Paestum (Poseidonia) in southern Italy.

New temples in the colonies were usually built on

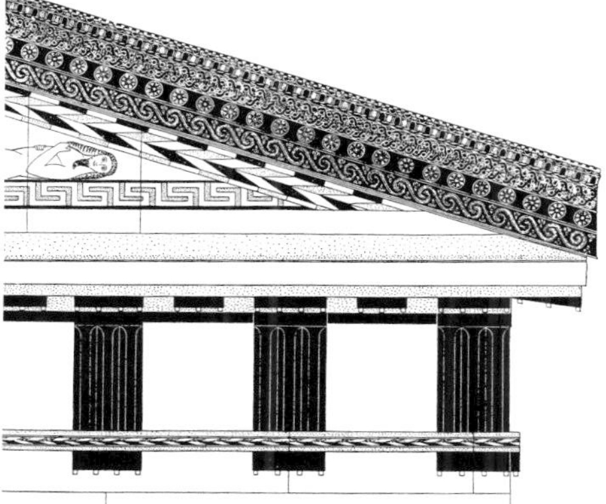

28 **Corfu, Temple of Artemis** c. 580 BC, restoration of west pediment and entablature.

Especially noteworthy is the appearance of the so-called Greek key pattern with the Minoan rosette and spiral wave. The latter is clearly the origin of the 'Vitruvian wave'.

On a stylobate 23.5 by 49 metres (77 by 161 feet) were eight by 17 columns. Though little is left on the site, it seems that the walls of the cella and the two rows of columns dividing it into nave and aisles were aligned with the four central columns of the front, giving a pteron the width of two intercolumniations.

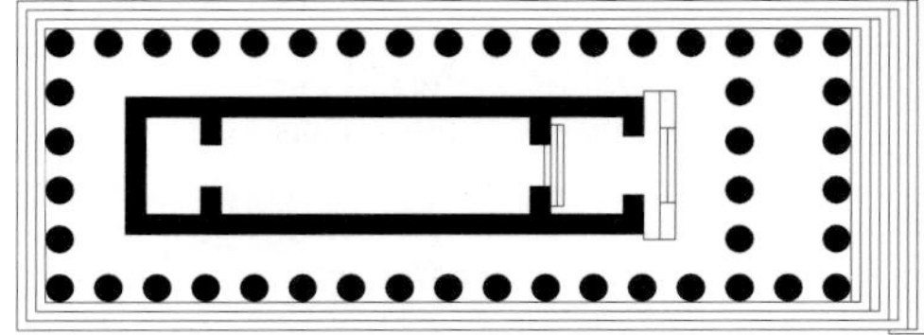

29 **Selinus (Selinunte), Sicily, Temple C** c. 550 BC, plan.

On a stylobate 23.9 by 63.7 metres (78 feet 6 inches by 209 feet) – a ratio of 1:2.66 – were six by 17 columns, 1.83 to 1.9 by 8.64 metres (6 feet to 6 feet 3 inches by 28 feet 4 inches), giving proportions of 1:4.78 to 1:4.53. For what was to be the last significant time in Sicily, the columns of the sides were more closely spaced than those of the ends. Following Ionic examples, the porch was preceded by a deep space divided by a second row of columns – that is, it had columns prostyle rather than in antis. Though carefully terminated opposite the fifth columns of the sides, the walls of the porch, cella and adytum were not aligned with any of the front columns, but with the second intercolumniations. Freeing the width of the cella from dependence on the colonnade of the front meant that its dimensions could be determined by the timbers available to roof it without internal supports.

new sites in the vicinity of the old ones – as at Acragas, Selinus and Paestum. Paestum has the most complete archaic Doric remains, a range that offers a particularly instructive comparison. The Temple of Hera I[30–31] (c. 530 BC) was prophetic in its pteron of nine by 18 columns, but its great width could not be roofed without the primitive central row of supports blocking the main axis. The Temple of Athena to the north (c. 520 BC)[33–34] represents the degree to which the colonies were advanced in planning while still archaic in their unconventional attitudes to the Order: Doric and Ionic were evidently mixed. Beside it, the almost complete Temple of Hera II – 'Poseidon', c. 460 BC (see 44–45, pages 107–09) – acknowledges the apogee of Doric recently attained at Olympia (see 42, pages 102–03).

Continual rethinking of the relationship of the parts to one another and to the whole, and even of the shape of the whole, is clearly apparent across the generations spanned by the temples at Paestum.[35] As at the Olympian Heraeum (see 26, page 69), the proportions at first are much stockier and tougher and the capital broader and flatter, representing the idea of cushioning in a more literal way.[32] Some 70 years later, all the elements have been brought into a tauter relationship.

30 **Paestum, (Poseidonia), southern Italy, Temple of Hera I ('Basilica')** c. 530 BC, interior from the west.

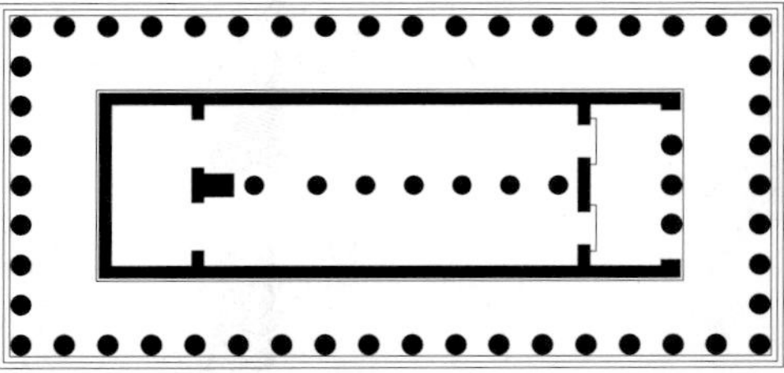

31 **Paestum, Temple of Hera I** plan.

On a stylobate 24.5 by 54.3 metres (80 feet 6 inches by 178 feet) – a ratio of 1:2.21 – the nine by 18 external and seven by 16 internal columns were 1.45 by 6.43 metres (4 feet 9 inches by 21 feet 1 inch), a ratio of 1:4.47.

An odd number of columns distinguishes the ends of several temples at Sicilian sites, and as in several later Sicilian works the columns on the ends here are set closer together than those on the sides except for the end bays of the latter, next to the corners. The alignment of the pronaos with the third column of the flanking colonnades, giving a wide pteron, is in line with near-contemporary practice at Selinus. The Ionic scale suggests a familiarity with the Temple of Artemis at Corfu – though the logic of the latter's octostyle plan (eight by 17 columns) apparently eluded the Italians.

32 **Paestum, Temple of Hera I** detail of capital.
Exaggerated entasis and diminution in the upper diameter of the columns were countered by the exceptionally broad, flat echinus. The underside of the latter was chased with ornament instead of annulets and the deep necking beneath it was incised with leaves.

33 **Paestum, Temple of Athena (Demeter)** c. 520 BC.

34 **Paestum, Temple of Athena** plan.

On a stylobate 14.53 by 32.87 metres (47 feet 8 inches by 107 feet 10 inches) – a ratio of 1:2.26 – were six by 13 columns of 1.27 by 6.12 metres (4 feet 2 inches by 20 feet 1 inch), giving proportions of 1:4.84. There was a prostyle portico but neither opisthodomos nor adytum.

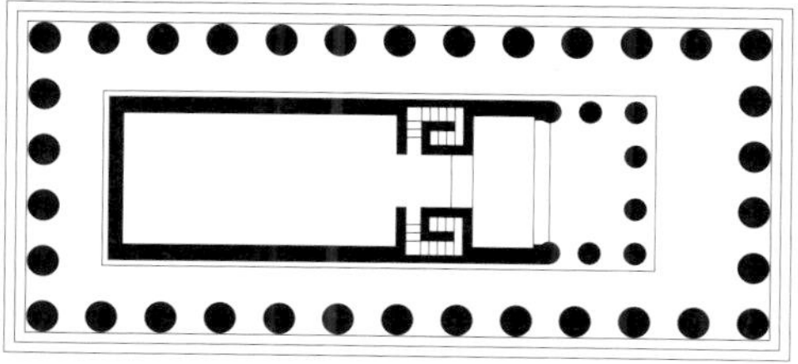

As in the Temple of Hera I, there was considerable decorative elaboration of the Doric capitals, especially the introduction of a florid neck and lower band to the echinus. The remains of the pronaos Order have Ionic characteristics. Without corona and shorn of mutules, the cornice was reduced to an Ionic egg-and-dart ovolo. A similar moulding replaced the regulae and guttae below the Doric frieze. The end metopes of each side were left wider than the others by the failure to adjust the spacing of the corner columns to accord with the displacement of the outer triglyphs from their centres. Coffered eaves were carried all around the temple in place of the usual Doric cornice of mutules, and bent up over the ends to form the pediments.

35 **Paestum** view from the Temple of Hera I through the Temple of Hera II ('Poseidon', c. 460 BC) to the Temple of Athena.

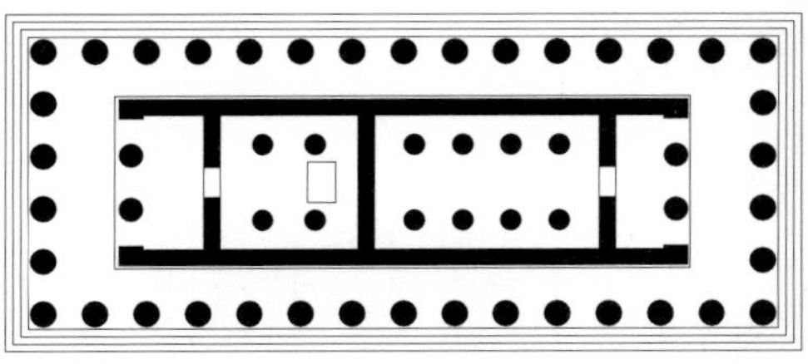

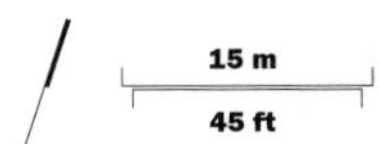

36 **Corinth, Temple of Apollo** plan.

The six by 15 columns stood on a stylobate 21.5 by 53.9 metres (70 feet 6 inches by 176 feet 11 inches) – a ratio of 1:2.5. The columns of the front were 1.74 by 7.24 metres (5 feet 8½ inches by 23 feet 9 inches), giving proportions of 1:4.15. The distance between their centres was 4.03 metres (13 feet 2½inches) – a ratio of axial spacing to base diameter of 2.31:1 and of axial spacing to column height of

Refinements of proportions and plan

While refining the proportions of the human form and its abstraction for the Order, the Greeks were also refining their conception of the proper ordering of the plan. The great length of buildings like the Heraeum at Samos (see 9, page 23) had been modified and the ratio of end to side adjusted at Olympia (see 26, page 69), but the irrational ratio of six columns at the ends and 15 columns at the sides (6:15) was sustained as the norm in major later archaic works such as the Temples of Apollo at Corinth (c. 540 BC)[36–37] and Delphi (c. 525 BC),[38] which incorporate a room beyond the cella (adytum) in addition to a porch and opisthodomos. Here archaic terracotta had ceded to stone or marble – carved in partial relief in the

1:1.8. The diameters of the columns and the spacing between them were reduced on the sides. The spacing was further reduced on the corners, as in the Heraeum at Olympia (see 26, page 69). In response to the columns of the pronaos and opisthodomos, the flanking walls extended from the cella to terminate in shallow returns (ante). The echinus, restrained in its bulge, was in a tauter relationship to the column than hitherto and there was no entasis.

37 **Corinth, Temple of Apollo** c. 540 BC, view of the acropolis with the remains of the temple.

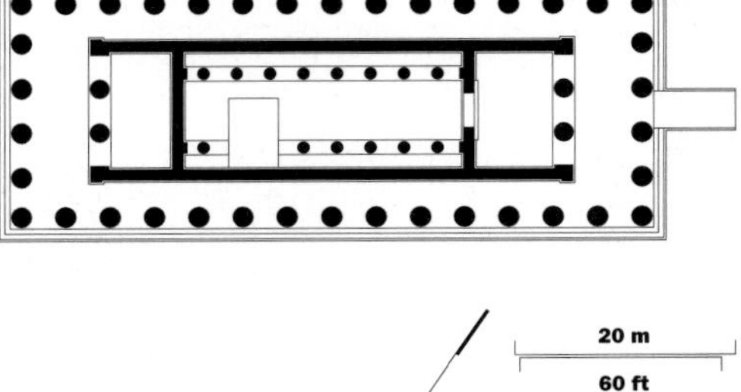

38 **Delphi, Temple of Apollo** built in place of several predecessors in the last quarter of the 6th century BC, destroyed by earthquake in 373 BC and rebuilt (with modified Order) after 366 BC, plan and elevation.

The six by 15 columns stood on a stylobate 21.7 by

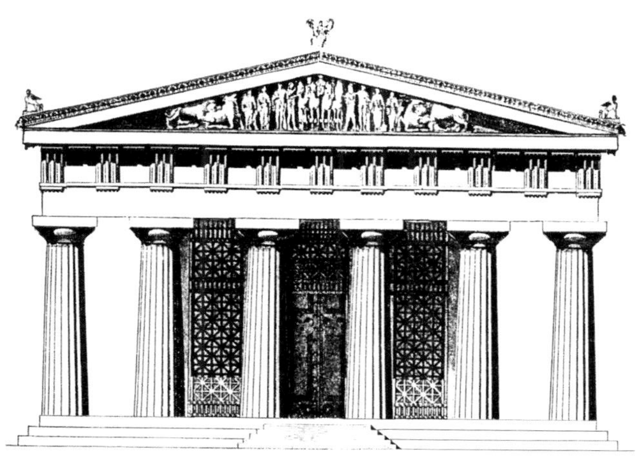

58.2 metres (71 feet 1 inch by 190 feet 10 inches) – a ratio of 1:2.68. The structure was largely of limestone, but the east end was executed in marble at the expense of the Athenian reformer Cleisthenes after 513 BC to woo to his cause those in attendance on the oracle.

metopes and in three full dimensions in the pediments – and the visual impact of the temple was immeasurably enhanced.

To counter optical illusion and enhance vitality, strict rectangularity and regularity were avoided in the main elements of the design. As at Olympia and Paestum, columns were tapered from bottom to top and their sides given a gentle bulge (entasis) to avoid the appearance of splaying and waisting, though this is less exaggerated in later archaic works on the mainland. A subtle upward curvature was introduced to the stylobate and this was naturally reflected in the entablature. First apparent in the Temple of Apollo at Corinth, this was doubtless originally designed for drainage, but was soon recognised as useful in counteracting the illusion of sagging in extended parallel horizontals separated by repeated verticals. Similarly the narrowing of the intercolumniations at each corner was originally devised to sustain a regularity of rhythm in the frieze when the end triglyphs were moved outwards from their proper place over the centre of the supporting column. However, it was also recognised that this countered the illusion that slender verticals seen against a void – like the corner columns against the sky – are further apart than those seen against a solid, like the cella walls.

Truth versus appearance

Despite the recognition that reason had sometimes to cede to sensation, at the end of the 6th century BC irrational ratios were rejected for the 1:2 ideal appreciable in pure geometry. In the Temple of Aphaea built on the island of Aegina c. 500 BC,[39] two squares are combined as the base for a pteron of six by 12 columns. Given a height:base diameter ratio of 5.3:1, internal columns high enough to carry the ceiling of the cella would have taken up most of the floor, so two orders were superimposed.

On its realisation at Aegina, the ideal was found wanting. The eye cannot register more than eight elements at once. So the eye could read the six end columns as a unit but not the greater number of side columns; the corner column, common to both ranges, assimilated itself to the end, leaving the side apparently short of a unit. Having spent centuries questing after the ideal and finding it in proportion and rational geometry, the Greeks were now confronted by a dis-

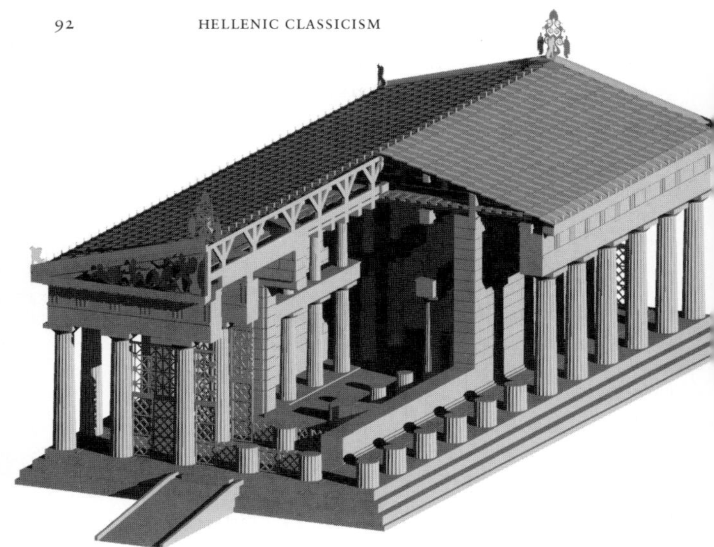

39 **Aegina, Temple of Aphaea** c. 500 BC, cutaway axonometric and worm's-eye view (OVERLEAF).

On a stylobate 13.8 by 28.8 metres (45 feet 2 inches by 94 feet 6 inches) – a ratio of 1:2.1 – the six by 12 columns were 0.99 by 5.26 metres (3 feet 3 inches by 17 feet 3 inches), giving proportions of 1:5.32, except for the slightly thicker corner ones. The axial spacing was 2.6 metres (8 feet 7 inches) on the front – a ratio of 2.65:1 and 1:2.01 to base diameter and column height respectively – and slightly narrower on the sides.

Of stuccoed limestone with marble pediment sculpture, the temple was built in place of an earlier work which was distyle in antis. The sequence of spaces was conventional, except for an off-centre door between the opisthodomos and the cella. The superimposed Doric Orders supporting the roof and dividing the cella into nave and aisles tapered in line with one another. Galleries were inserted over the aisles on the intermediate architrave, but since there was no frieze at this level, these do not seem to have been part of the original design.

Abandoning the archaic practice of making all the columns of each end thicker than those of the sides, the architect here thickened only the corner columns – to counter their apparent attrition when seen against the void

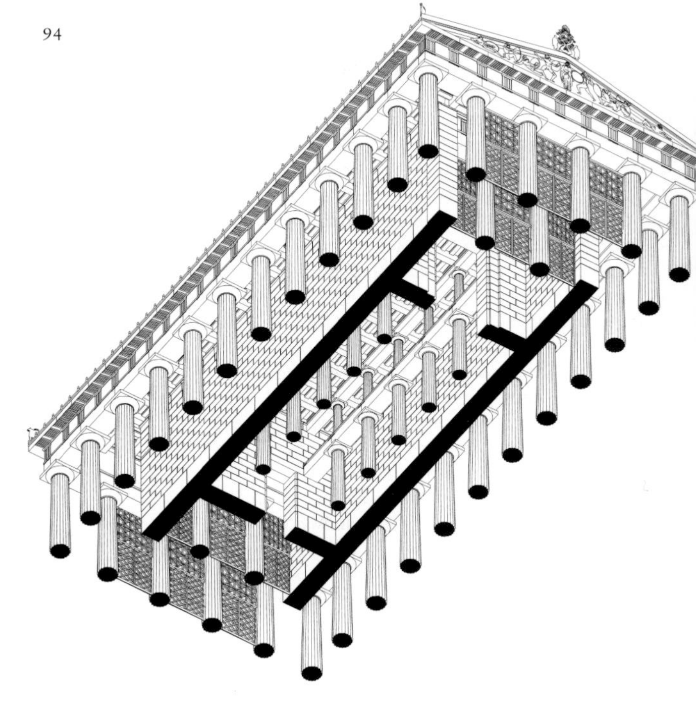

crepancy between what reason dictated and what seemed right to the eye. They had to make the extraordinary psychological leap of denying Truth for the sake of appearance. To cope with this problem of optical illusion they reverted to the irrational: the next generation of temples had one more column to each side than twice the number on the ends – usually 13:6 – a precedent set in the late 6th-century BC Temple of Athena Pronea at Delphi and the Temples of Athena at Paestum (see 34, page 81) and at Assos (c. 540 BC, a rare Doric temple in Asia Minor).

of the sky, and to enhance the overall sense of stability. The impression – given by the heavy horizontal entablature bearing down on a regular series of slender verticals – that the façades splayed out at the top was obviated by the inward inclination of the columns of the sides.

The precinct, earlier than the present temple, preserves rare remains of a late archaic propylaeum. With two porches back to back, each with two columns in antis and matching in size, it clearly originates in the Mycenaean form of the bit-hilani without flanking towers – like the entrance to 'Temple I' at Hattusas (see volume I, ORIGINS, page 169.)

The ideal human form

By the beginning of the 5th century BC the Dorians had also arrived at the set of proportions for the human figure which was to be considered canonical: a standard approximating the ideal. In the 'Strangford Apollo',[40] the relationship of the various parts of the body to one another and to the whole has been idealised. So perfect is this figure in its symmetry, representing timeless truth rather than transitory appearance, that it inspires no feelings: it is dead. The divine ideal abstracted from man denied the gods something manifest in man: life. How was this extra dimension of vitality to be represented within a perfect form? Vitality implied movement and movement by its very nature would upset the ideal balance between the parts drawn from coherent proportions and the rational organisation in terms of symmetry.

Mastering perspective and abandoning the convention of the characteristic view with the foreshortening of limbs in the representation of transitory states, Hellenic painters and sculptors – probably first in Ionia –

40 **Kouros, 'Strangford Apollo'** marble from Araphne, c. 500 BC (London, British Museum).

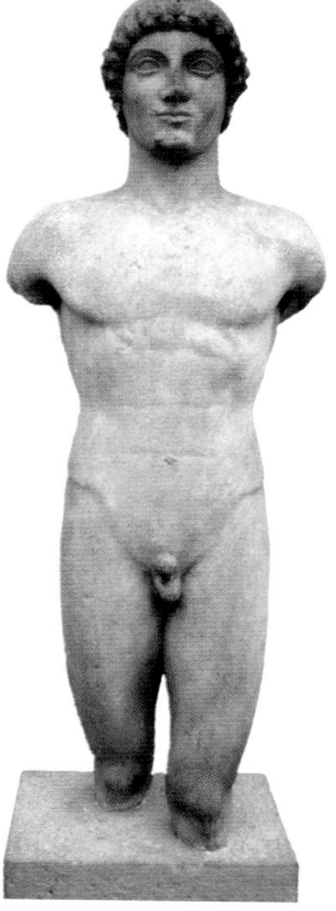

41 **Polycleitus: Doryphoros** Roman marble copy (Naples, National Museum).

Polycleitus is generally considered to have been a contemporary of Phidias, and the Doryphoros was probably produced after 450 BC. The original is lost, but the comparison of surviving copies and fragments suggests that this one in Naples, recovered from Pompeii and therefore dating from before AD 79, is among the most accurate.

Pliny, who reports Polycleitus as active later in the century, quotes Varro (1st century BC) as characterising the Doryphoros as 'foursquare'. Galen (the 2nd-century AD medical writer) quotes Chrysippus (3rd-century BC Stoic) as maintaining that 'beauty consists in the symmetry not of the elements but of the numbers ... of finger to finger and of all these to hand and wrist, and of those to forearm, of forearm to arm and of all to all, as it is written in Polycleitus' *Canon*.' From this descends the idea that beauty depends on the complete co-ordination of all the parts so that nothing may be added or subtracted without spoiling the whole.

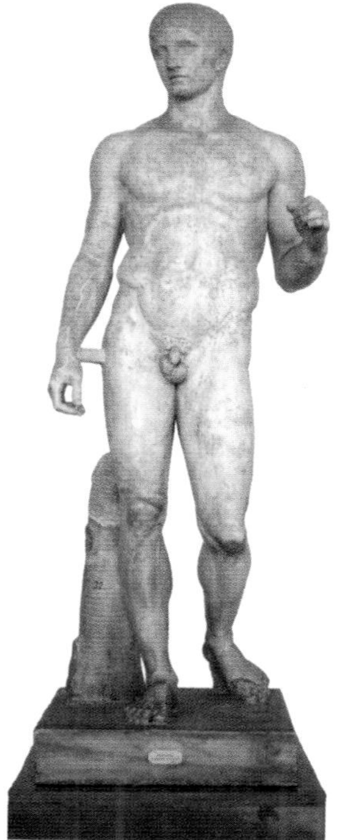

found divine stasis not in motionlessness but in equilibrium. The culminating achievement in the mainland was the Doryphoros of Polycleitus, c. 450 BC.[41] Here, in the cycle of movements preparatory to throwing a spear, the athlete's limbs have been caught in a moment of asymmetrical balance.

Polycleitus wrote a book called the *Canon* to transmit the ideal proportions of his athletes and the formula for achieving their celebrated equipoise. Without the text or the original statue, it is difficult to reconstruct his ideas precisely. Ancient commentators describe the figure as 'foursquare', and it is clear from Roman copies that it matched the weight of the mature Doric Order. As to the formula, copies of the statue reveal that it requires the balancing out of forces across the body: the leg bearing the weight of the body is counterbalanced on the other side by the active arm; the other arm and the opposite leg are in relaxation. Tension and relaxation, the straight and the bent, are counterposed. The key lies in plotting the centre of gravity, as distinct from the given centre of a symmetrical form, and since the essential element is irrational, success depends on intricate adjustments inspired by the genius of the artist and the keen eye of the observer. Stemming from the study of perspective, Polycleitus' formula for balanced asymmetry was to be enduringly influential on sculpture and architecture.

The apogee of the Doric temple

Designed by Libon of Elis, the Temple of Zeus at Olympia[42] – begun c. 470 BC and enshrining Phidias' image of the Olympian ruler (see 4, page 15) – anticipates Polycleitus' synthesis of weight and suppleness. Whereas hitherto the dimensions of the cella were established first, leaving those of the peristyle dependent, here the procedure was reversed and the essential measurements throughout the building were derived from the common denominator of the intercolumniation, any variation from which was calculated to counter optical illusion. While the main parts were all in the ratio of 1:2, the irrational ratio of 6:13 between the columns on the ends and those on the sides took account of perspective foreshortening. The curvature of all the main lines countered optical illusion with vitality. At 1:4.7, the proportions of the column are hardly those of the athlete, but certainly match his combination of strength and virility in spirit.

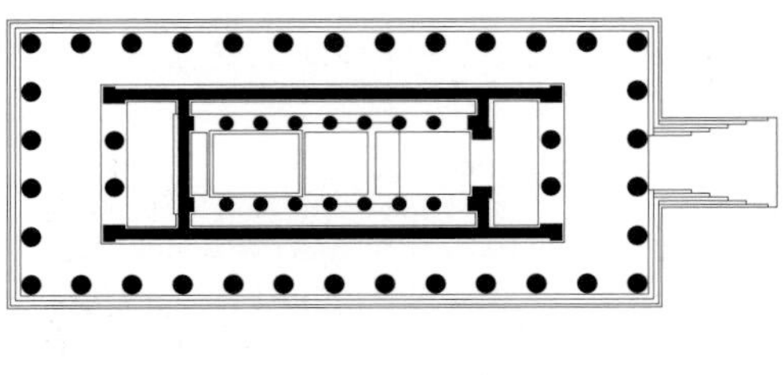

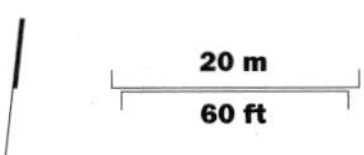

42 **Olympia, Temple of Zeus** c. 470 BC, plan and elevation.

On a stylobate 27.7 by 64.1 metres (90 feet 10 inches by 210 feet 4 inches) – a ratio of 1:2.32 – the six by 13 columns were 2.26 by 10.44 metres (7 feet 5 inches by 34 feet 3 inches), giving proportions of 1:4.64, on the front and slightly thinner on the sides, where they were all inclined inwards to counter apparent splaying, as at the Temple of

Aphaea at Aegina (see 39, pages 92–94). The axial spacing was 5.25 metres (17 feet 2¾ inches) on the front – a ratio of 2.32:1 and 1:2 to base diameter and column height respectively – and minutely narrower on the sides. In Doric feet, the height of the columns was 32, the intercolumniations 16, the width of the abacus and the spacing of the triglyphs 8, the spacing of the mutules and lion-head spouts 4, and so on.

One of the largest Doric temples in mainland Greece, the structure was of the local coarse limestone covered with marble plaster coloured in accordance with convention (see 14, page 42). The sculpture was in Parian marble. The groups in the two pediments (the contest for the Peloponnesus between the Achaean invader Pelops and the incumbent Oenomaus on the east and the battle of Lapiths and Centaurs, representing the triumph of the Hellenes over barbarism, on the west) were more carefully calculated to fit their triangular fields than ever before. Masterly too was the concentration of the high-relief sculptures, representing the labours of Hercules, in the square fields of the frieze metopes over the back and front porticos within the peristyle. The metopes of the front portico bore shields. Phidias' statue of Olympian Zeus (see 4, page 15), inserted some years after the completion of the building between the columns which divided nave from aisles and supported an interpolated gallery in the cella, drew maximum dramatic impact by overfilling its space.

43 **Selinus, Temple of Hera ('E')** c. 460 BC, view from the south-west.

On a stylobate 25.3 by 67.7 metres (83 feet by 222 feet) – a ratio of 1:2.67 – the six by 15 columns were 2.26 by 10.13 metres (7 feet 5 inches by 33 feet 3 inches), giving proportions of 1:4.48. The axial spacing was 4.7 metres (15 feet 6 inches) – a ratio of 2.08:1 and 1:2.15 to base diameter and column height respectively. Departing from precedent, variation at the corners was insignificant. The temple was destroyed by earthquake; the remains have been reconstructed.

Unfortunately the great temple at Olympia was destroyed in an earthquake, but the near-contemporary Temples of Hera at Selinus[43] and Paestum[44–46] are substantially intact. The colonists of Paestum had done extremely well in the Olympic Games of 460 BC and thanked their patron deity with a temple inspired by the great Olympian work. The result, however, is conservatively long – as at Selinunte – and the proportions of the Order are conservatively stocky.

Our best image of a Doric temple is provided by the Hephaesteum (Temple of Athena and Hephaestus) in Athens,[47] and it is this work which took the Doric Order to its apogee, though it may be seen as over-refined. Begun in 449 BC, just before the Parthenon, it followed the Olympian example in plan except inside the cella, but its proportions of 1:5.61 were nearly Polycleitan and posed an inescapable problem for the future development of the Doric Order: was further slenderness compatible with its nature? The architects of the Parthenon thought not.

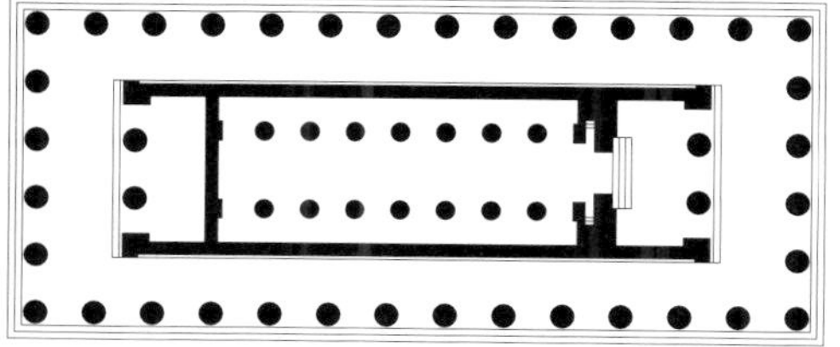

44 **Paestum, Temple of Hera II** c. 460 BC, plan.

On a stylobate 24.3 by 60 metres (79 feet 7 inches by 196 feet 9 inches) – a ratio of 1:2.47 – the six by 14 columns were 2.11 metres by 8.88 metres (6 feet 11 inches by 29 feet 1½ inches), giving proportions of 1:4.2, on the front and slightly narrower on the sides. The axial spacing was 4.47 metres (14 feet 8 inches) on the front – a ratio of 2.12:1 and 1:1.99 to base diameter and column height respectively – and slightly wider on the sides except where, following Sicilian precedents, the penultimate bays were narrowed in conformity with the bays on either side of each corner. Following mainland practice after the Temple of Aphaea at Aegina (see 39, pages 92–94), the interior was divided and the roof joists supported by twin colonnades of two superimposed, consistently tapered Doric Orders. The lower Order had an architrave but no frieze and there were no galleries. The internal staircase served the roof.

45 **Paestum, Temple of Hera II** view from east-south-east.

46 **Paestum, Temple of Hera II** interior.

47 **Athens, Hephaesteum (Temple of Athena and Hephaestus)** c. 449 BC, view from the south.

On a stylobate 13.7 by 31.8 metres (45 feet by 104 feet 3 inches) – a ratio of 1:2.32 – the six by 13 columns were 1.01 metres by 5.71 metres (3 feet 4 inches by 18 feet 9 inches), giving proportions of 1:5.61. The axial spacing was 2.59 metres (8 feet 5¾ inches) – a ratio of 2.54:1 and 1:2.21 to base diameter and column height respectively.

The plan was conventional – except for the return of the internal colonnade around the west end of the cella – with a single column on the main axis behind the cult images and the careful alignment of the pronaos ante with the third column of the sides. The external frieze was regular too, but only the metopes of the front and the first two intercolumniations before the pronaos were embellished with relief sculpture. The Doric columns of the pronaos and opisthodomos carried Ionic friezes with continuous narratives in high relief, the eastern one extending across to the peristyle further to emphasise the space before the pronaos. Like the columns of the pteron, the columns of the pronaos and opisthodomos were exceptionally slender. This is crucial as the entablature was relatively higher than usual.

The proportions of the Order were designed to counter perspective foreshortening of the east front in the main view from the agora below. Over-refinement may be sensed in the unknown architect's incorporation of all the optical-illusion controls developed by his predecessors to enhance the sense of strength and vitality. Variations from standard dimensions include contracting the corner bays and thickening the corner columns, inclination of the vertical lines, and the curvature of the verticals and horizontals. Moreover, this was the first Doric temple to be built entirely of Pentalic marble.

The same architect is credited with the similar, slightly later, Temple of Poseidon at Sunium. Also viewed primarily from below, the proportions of its columns were even slenderer (1:5.78).

Athens reached the height of her power and prosperity under Pericles (c. 495–429 BC), who in 447 BC refounded the Parthenon, inaugurating the transformation of the Acropolis following its devastation by the Persians a generation earlier. In addition to the Parthenon, the project involved completely rebuilding the gate-house – the Propylaea – and the temple complex known as the Erechtheum, as well as the founding of several entirely new works and the restoration of surviving fragments.[48] At least three great architects were involved: Ictinus, Callicrates and Mnesicles.

The Parthenon (Temple of Athena Polias)

The success of the Parthenon – one of the most admired buildings of all time – is due to the collaboration of Ictinus, supported by Callicrates, with Phidias, one of the greatest sculptors of all time. If the apogee of the male Order was achieved by Libon of Elis at Olympia (see 42, pages 102–03) and surpassed by the Hephaesteum in Athens (see 47, pages 112–13), the architects of the Parthenon eclipsed it. Incorporating Ionic elements, their work is eclectic. It is no accident that the Orders were crossed in Athens, where Achaeans intermingled with Aegeans on their way to the islands and Ionia.

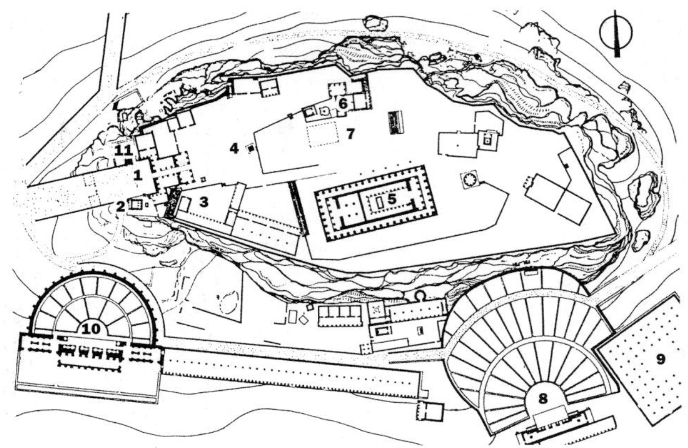

48 **Athens, Acropolis** plan and model.

(1) Propylaea; (2) Temple of Nike; (3) sanctuary of Artemis; (4) statue of Athena Promachos; (5) Temple of Athena Polias (Parthenon) and probable site of earlier Temple of Athena Polias (so-called Hundred-Foot Temple or Hecatompedon), c. 566 BC; (6) Temple of Athena Polias with shrine for Poseidon-Erechtheus (Erechtheum); (7) site

of earlier Erechtheum; (8) Theatre of Dionysius and (9) odeon; (10) Roman odeon; (11) so-called pedestal of Agrippa (in fact erected by Eumenes II of Pergamon in 178 BC to support votive sculpture).

49 **Athens, Acropolis, Parthenon**

447–432 BC, view from west-south-west.

The architects saw cross-fertilisation between Doric and Ionic as the solution to specific design problems. A front of eight columns, unprecedented in mainland Doric buildings, was common in Ionia: in the Parthenon, the extra width accommodated the great chryselephantine statue of the deity (in this case Athena) more easily than in the Temple of Zeus at Olympia (see 4, page 15), though the proportions established there are preserved in the Parthenon's peristyle of eight by 17 columns.[49–50] In addition to porch and opisthodomos, antechamber and cella, a special room was needed for the treasury – the 'Parthenon' which gave its name to the building. In the cella there was room for the usual superimposition of columns to provide intermediate support for the roof. In the restricted space of the treasury, this would have looked cluttered,

50 **Athens, Acropolis, Parthenon** section and plan.
On a stylobate of 30.9 by 69.5 metres (101 feet 4 inches by 228 feet) – a ratio of 1:2.25 or 4:9 – the eight by 17 columns were 1.9 metres (6 feet 3 inches) by 10.44 metres (34 feet 3 inches), giving proportions of 1:5.48. The axial spacing was 4.29 metres (14 feet 1 inch) except for the corner bays, which were more than usually contracted,

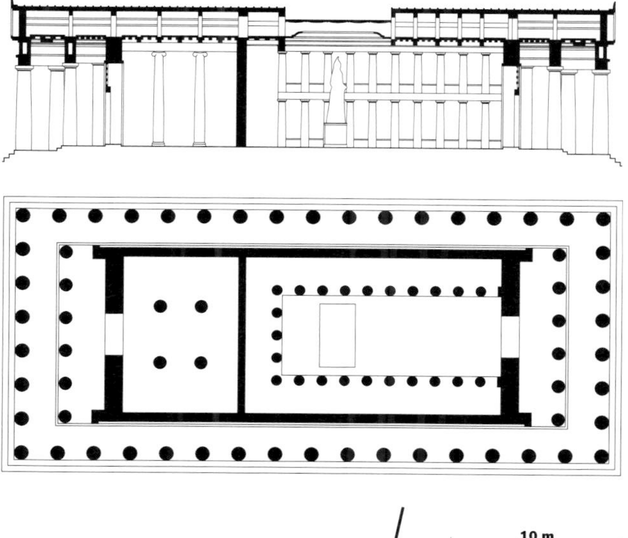
10 m
30 ft

apparently in response to the greater width of the façade. The ratio of base diameter to inter-axial width and of the width of the pteron to the total height of the Order was 1:2.25 or 4:9.

Ictinus and Callicrates used the platform and much of the material prepared for a project begun c. 488 BC and destroyed by the Persians in 480, but their new work was shorter and wider – in accordance with the canon of proportions established in the Temple of Zeus at Olympia (see 42, pages 102–03) and to accommodate Phidias' statue of Athena. Pronaos and opisthodomos were reduced to shallow porticos but had the greater width of six columns standing free of the contracted ante (prostyle hexastyle). It was here that the Doric Order ceded its triglyphs and metopes to Phidias' great Ionic frieze.

The metopes of the peristyle were graded in increasing width from the sides to the centre. The proportions of the capital were varied as building progressed from west to south, north and east to obviate excessive stiffness, the abacus becoming wider and the echinus more generously curved. The superimposed Doric colonnades in the cella returned parallel to the west wall to form an ambulatory behind Phidias' image of the goddess. The adytum beyond was accessible only from the opisthodomos.

while a single canonical Doric Order rising from the ground would have taken up most of the floor space. The slender Ionic provided the solution.

Following the Panathenaic procession (held every four years to endow the cult statue of Athena with a new robe) in flowing movement around the cella walls, Phidias' celebrated frieze[51] is Ionic – in contrast with the episodic zoning of the traditional Doric metopes of the external pteron.[52] And as Phidias lightened the proportions established by his predecessors in the figures of his frieze – approximating those of Polycleitus' *Canon* and generating a flowing movement from the formula for balanced asymmetry – so too Ictinus lightened the proportions of his Order to 1:5.48, though not quite as much as in the Athenian Hephaesteum (see 47, pages 112–13).

Sculpture and structure were white marble with the details lavishly coloured – in line with general practice rather than as a specific manifestation of Ionic sensuality.[53] The temple is celebrated for its sophisticated range of optical-correction devices: all were anticipated elsewhere, but the costly precision craftsmanship here clearly furthered Ionic conceptions of visual significance.[54]

51 **Athens, Acropolis, Parthenon** detail of Phidias' frieze. The frieze represents the Panathenaic procession held every four years to endow the cult statue of Athena with a new robe (London, British Museum).

52 **Athens, Acropolis, Parthenon** detail of south-west corner showing outer pteron, opisthodomos and Ionic frieze carried on the portico columns and cella walls.

53 **Athens, Acropolis, Parthenon** reconstruction of east front.

The main structural elements – columns, architraves and coronas – which were stuccoed in white marble plaster over stone in most Doric temples were here the natural colour of the marble. Secondary – or originally protective – elements, such as the incisions at the top of the columns, triglyphs, regulae and mutules, were blue. The guttae were white and the horizontal tenia and via mouldings below and above the frieze were red and gold.

The sculpture was the natural colour of the marble – except for gilt-bronze detail – but the Panathenaic frieze, at least, had a blue background. In contrast with its low relief, the metopes were in exceptionally high relief. The pediment figures, even as fragments, rank among the supreme masterpieces of sculpture in the round. The metopes represented the battles of gods and giants on the east front, of Athenians and Amazons on the west, of Lapiths and Centaurs on the south side, and of Greeks and Trojans on the north. The east pediment was dedicated to the birth of Athena; the western one contained the contest of Athena and Poseidon for Attica.

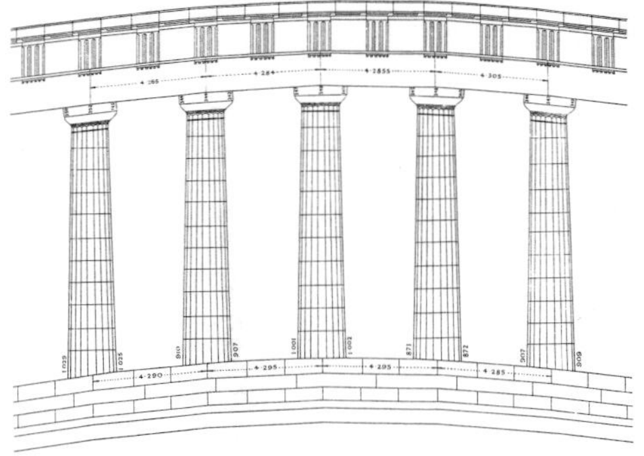

54 **Athens, Acropolis, Parthenon** diagram of colonnade exaggerating the devices designed to control optical illusion.

No other building has had its strength and vitality enhanced at greater cost through the subtle combination of curves and inclinations of horizontals and verticals. Yet all the optical controls employed by Ictinus were invented by his predecessors.

(1) End bays had been contracted to cope with the displacement of the triglyphs since the early archaic period – as in the Heraeum at Olympia (see 26, page 69). This also lent

the appearance of greater strength at the corners and obviated the apparent attrition of columns seen against the light of the sky rather than against the mass of the cella walls. Corner-bay contraction here was double the norm.

(2) Following the abandonment of the archaic practice of making all the columns of the ends thicker than those of the sides, attrition was countered and strength enhanced by thickening the corner columns – as in the Temple of Aphaea at Aegina (see 39, pages 92–94). The corner columns of the Parthenon were augmented by one-fortieth of the standard diameter. In the Hephaesteum (see 47, pages 112–13) it is one-fiftieth, as recommended by Vitruvius.

(3) The sense of attrition had been counteracted from the earliest archaic period by curving columns outwards (entasis). Often exaggerated until late in the 6th century BC, the refinement of this device marked the development of the Doric Order. The Parthenon's entasis expanded to 1.75 centimetres (11/16 inch) over the straight line drawn from column top to base. Expansion was just over 5 centimetres (2 inches) in the archaic Temple of Hera I at Paestum (see 30, pages 76–77).

(4) The upward curvature of horizontals in the later archaic period (as in the Temple of Apollo at Corinth) was perhaps first adopted to shed water, but it must also have

The Propylaea

Through the concessions he made to the Ionic, Ictinus demonstrated that the days of pure Doric were over: the flexible Ionic admitted of development; the rigid Doric did not. And in the Propylaea, too, Mnesicles looked to the Ionic for the solution to a problem unresolvable in Doric terms.

The outer and inner porticos are on different levels and the way rises through a waiting area between

been seen to counteract a sense of sagging and to enhance apparent vitality. The curvature of the Parthenon's stylobate produces a rise of 6 centimetres (2 3/8 inches) on the ends and 11 centimetres (4 5/16 inches) on the sides.

(5) The consistent inclination of vertical lines obviated the sense of splaying at the top for greater apparent stability – as first encountered in the Temple of Aphaea at Aegina (see 39, pages 92–94), though there, as in the Temple of Zeus at Olympia, only the side columns were inclined. In the Parthenon the pteron inclines inwards by 6 centimetres (2 3/8 inches).

55 **Athens, Acropolis, Propylaea** 437–432 BC, view of central passage and Ionic Order.

56 **Athens, Acropolis, Propylaea** view from the south-west.

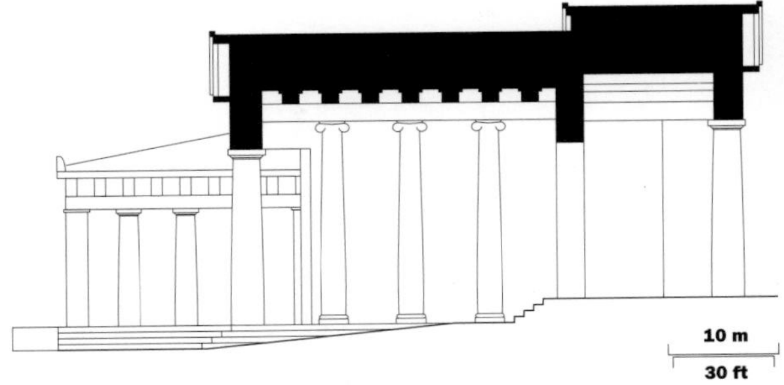

57 **Athens, Acropolis, Propylaea** section and plan showing projected and executed work.

Probably designed by Mnesicles, the Propylaea replaced an earlier structure demolished in 437 BC but remained incomplete after the outbreak of the Peloponnesian War in 431 BC.

The double portico of the Mycenaean type, facing west and east, was separated by a wall with three main doors and two posterns. The sacred way rose 1.75 metres (5 feet 9 inches) along its axis. Though the six Doric columns before each front had the same diameters (1.56 metres; 5 feet 1½ inches), at nearly 8.8 metres high (29 feet), the western ones – seen from below – were just under 0.3 metre (1 foot)

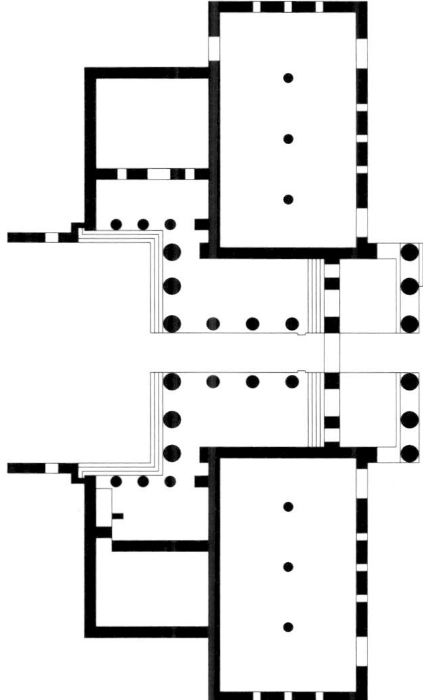

taller than the eastern ones. The central intercolumniation was wider than those of the sides, obviously to facilitate passage up the ramp which cut through the stylobate. The inner portico was shallow enough to be spanned in marble without intermediate support, but at more than twice the depth to shelter waiting visitors, the outer one needed internal supports. The two rows of three Ionic columns introduced here supported a marble ceiling which, spanning 5.5 metres (18 feet) over the aisles, remained a wonder even to Pausanias over 500 years later.

Halls planned to flank the eastern portico were never erected. Pendant wings were planned to project westward, with three columns in antis facing each other across the sacred way, but only the northern one was completed (as a picture gallery). The southern one, stopped short by the sanctuary of Artemis to its south-east, was left open to the west as a portico to the precinct of the Temple of Nike. The portico's south wall terminated opposite the outermost column of the temple's north side, beyond which was an isolated pier to effect symmetry with the north wing.

them.[55–57] Since the porticos were to be consistent in their dimensions, the columns in the intermediate zone – which rose from the level of the outer portico to support a flat ceiling approximating the height of the inner portico – obviously had to be taller than those of either portico. If they were Doric, they would also have to be thicker. To avoid discrepancy and the narrowing of the passageway, Mnesicles introduced the Ionic.

The Temple of Nike and the Erechtheum

The Periclean transformation of the Acropolis continued from 430 BC with the small Temple of Nike,[58] on a promontory west of the Propylaea, and the shrine for Poseidon-Erechtheus (Erechtheum),[59–61] both probably the work of Callicrates. The former is an orthodox prostyle tetrastyle building. The latter is extraordinary: diversified in its plan to incorporate several sacred sites, it was built on various levels – a problem which would have been extremely difficult to handle within the restrictions of the Doric proportional system.

These two works came as close as any building, other than the later Temple of Athena Polias at

58 **Athens, Acropolis, Temple of Nike** 427 BC, view from the east.

Conceived by Callicrates on a larger scale in 449 BC, the Temple of Nike was erected from 427 BC to reduced plans – 5.4 by 8.2 metres (17 feet 8 inches by 26 feet 9 inches) at its base – accommodating it to the smaller site left by the construction of the Propylaea in the meantime. The pronaos was dispensed with in favour of a shallow portico (prostyle tetrastyle) and the cella was diminished to a virtual square beyond screens between piers in antis. A matching portico was applied before the blind west wall.

The proportions of the Order (1:7.82) were unusually stocky for Ionic. The Attic form of base achieved its exquisite canonical form, with a single scotia separated by two torus mouldings, the lower one broader than the upper one. The work as built retained the familiar tripartite architrave rather than the single one in the building as originally planned. The magnificent frieze represented episodes from the Battle of Plataea.

59 **Athens, Acropolis, Erechtheum**
420–405 BC, view from the south-east.

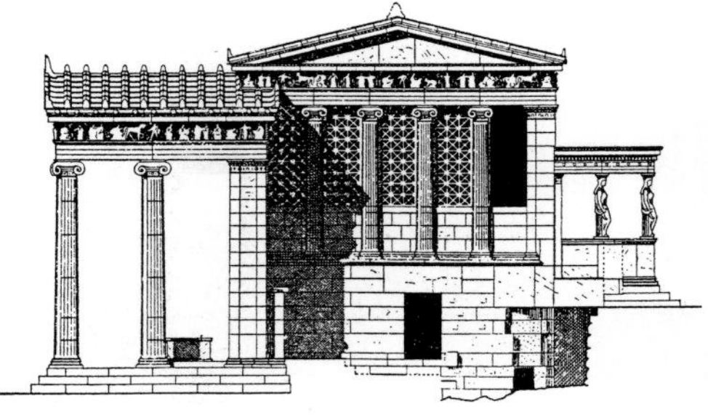

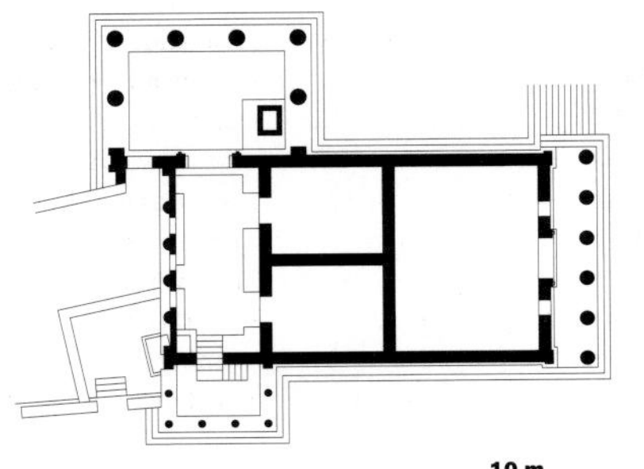
10 m
30 ft

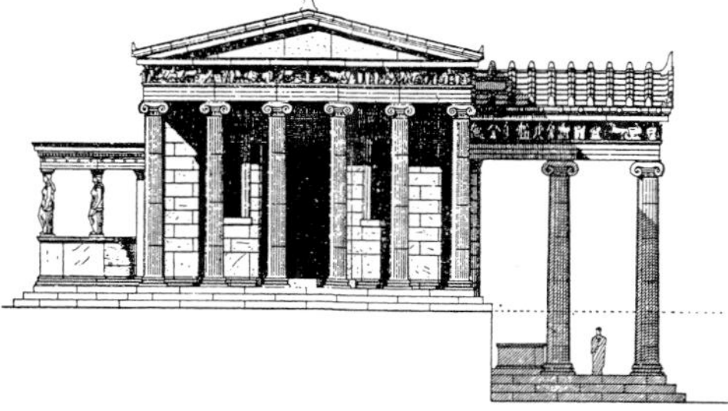

60 **Athens, Acropolis, Erechtheum** elevations and plan.

The earlier Erechtheum complex, to the south of the Periclean one, was rebuilt by the Peisistratids (tyrants of Athens from 561–510 BC). Surrounded by a Doric peristyle of six by 12 columns, it had Ionic porticos to the pronaos and opisthodomos from which a continuous Ionic frieze extended around the cella. The building was of limestone but the sculpture was of marble throughout and included pedimental groups carved in the round for perhaps the first time. Badly damaged by the Persians in 480, the peristyle and the eastern half of the cella, containing the shrine to Athena, were demolished. The rest may have been converted into a treasury.

Superseding the Peisistratid work, which had provided a precedent for mixing the Doric and Ionic Orders, the present Erechtheum was built from 420–405 BC on a split-level site to the north of the old one. The architect had to rehouse Athena Polias on the upper level and provide for Erechtheus on the lower level. He also had to shelter the sacred marks made by Poseidon's trident in the contest for Attica with Athena without harming the latter's sacred olive tree immediately to the west.

Athena Polias was given a rectangular cella behind the eastern portico (prostyle hexastyle). The lower level to the west was subdivided for the cult of Erechtheus by screens which did not reach the full height of the space. This area was entered from the west, through the compound of Athena's tree. To provide height for the door, the western colonnade was raised over a substantial basement. Evidently displaced further east than originally planned at the insistence of those responsible for Athena's tree, the six columns of this front were attached in whole or part to a screen wall with three windows – perhaps a Roman addition. Both the caryatid portico to the south and the prostyle tetrastyle northern portico, sheltering the trident marks of Poseidon, overlapped the main block to the west. This last, extremely awkwardly placed, may have been intended originally to cover Athena's tree.

The Erechtheum was built of Pentalic marble, inset with

61 **Athens, Acropolis, Erechtheum, detail of architrave moulding** (London, British Museum).

Note in the background a fragment of the Temple of Augustus.

black stone behind the friezes. The height of the columns varied, with proportions ranging from 1:9 to 1:9.5. The door from the northern portico and the capitals throughout were exceptionally rich, with compound spiral volutes intertwined with a bronze fillet and an anthemion decoration. The architrave had the traditional three fascias and a sculpted frieze, but dentils were omitted from the cornice except on the southern portico. With their clothes falling in flute-like folds over the weight-bearing leg, the caryatids (see 59, page 140–41) are the supreme masterpieces of the genre.

Priene (see 19, page 54), to establishing a canon for the Greek Ionic. The variation in the proportions of their Orders from just under 1:8 in the Temple of Nike to 1:9.35 in the northern portico of the Erechtheum illustrates the flexibility of the Order. The first sign of the impact of this standard abroad has been detected in the Nereid Monument at Xanthus in Lycia.[62] The Order of this miniature temple has capitals and entablature that recall respectively those of the Erechtheum's northern portico and caryatid portico (see 59, pages 140–41). The coffered ceiling was modelled on that of the Propylaea.

62 **Xanthus, Lycia, so-called Nereid Monument** c. 410 BC, view of reconstruction (London, British Museum).

The small peripteral temple on its podium was a development of the traditional Lycian reproduction of a portable timber coffin as a sarcophagus with a gabled lid raised from the ground on a rectangular base. In addition to statues of nereids (nymphs) between the columns there were four friezes – two on the podium, another around the cella and the fourth on the architrave.

63 **Athens, Acropolis** view from the south-west.

The sanctuary of Dionysius

The Acropolis complex[63] was completed with the sanctuary of Dionysius at the foot of its south-eastern slope. This included a great theatre.[64] Along with the temple, the theatre was the most important Hellenic public building type – and one which also had a religious role to play, since drama furthered the cult of the gods. The theatre originated with choral dances associated with the cult of Dionysius, to which Thespis introduced an actor at Athens c. 534 BC.

The original dancing place (orchestra) was a circle of stamped earth. A raked timber structure must soon have been provided for the audience, but the collapse of such a structure in or near the Athenian agora some time during the 70th Olympiad (500–496 BC) prompted the development of the cult on the southern slopes of the Acropolis, where nature provided permanent tiered seating and a splendid view beyond the orchestral circle and the adjacent sanctuary. The proliferation of parts for actors after the age of Pericles prompted the development of facilities for them in a building erected beyond the orchestra. As this blocked the view, painted scenery was hung on it behind a low stage.

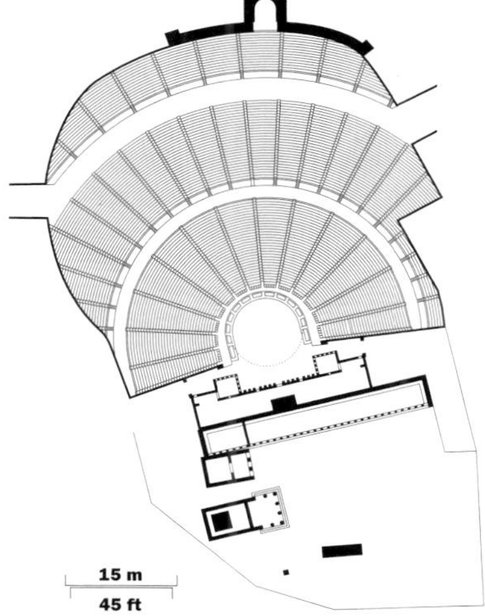

64 **Athens, Acropolis, sanctuary of Dionysius** plan.

When the theatre was first established on the southern slope of the Acropolis early in the 5th century BC the natural rock seating was supplemented in timber. The front banks of seats had been regularised in masonry before the end of the century. In the mid 4th century the theatre was enlarged to cover some 5600 square metres (60,000 square feet) and to accommodate 10,000 people. The semi-circle of the auditorium extended in two parallel banks, forming a 'U' about the orchestra.

The timber structure provided for the actors – located beyond the orchestra and hung with painted scenery – appeared early in the second half of the 5th century BC. This building was rebuilt about the turn of the century as a hall attached to the back of a stoa bordering the sanctuary. The new work had projecting wings (parascenium) framing a timber stage (proscenium) which was removed when not required. This temporary arrangement seems to have lasted until c. 150 BC.

Built to the east of the theatre, the music hall (odeon) was square with seats on three sides and a timber roof supported on nine rows of nine columns. The type was established for the shrine built for the mysteries of Demeter at Eleusis. The original building there seems to have had three rows of seven seats; seven rows of seven were projected in mid-century, but this was reduced in execution to six rows with a central lantern. The mysteries of Demeter and Dionysius were presumably not dissimilar, at least in their procedures.

The organisation of the site

Before considering the disposition of the great works on the Acropolis, we must return to the sanctuary of Zeus at Olympia.[65–66] An irregular space enclosed by a wall and centred on a sacred grove, the site shows no formal order in the relationship between the different elements. Even the two main buildings – the Heraeum and the Temple of Zeus – are slightly out of alignment with one another, while the small treasuries are not lined up in a neat row. Except in the much later works to the south and west, the discretion of each building is scrupulously respected. An appreciable sense of balance between the forms was doubtless effected by means of planting, masking disparity and allowing informal compositions to coalesce.

From the restoration of the Acropolis, it is certainly clear that when the Greeks related buildings to one another they did it visually – in accordance with Ionic sensitivity. An informal balance was achieved by adjusting the size, shape and weight of one mass vis-à-vis the other elements on the site about a centre of gravity – just as in the formula of Polycleitus. In the case of the Acropolis, some imagination applied to the characteristic view from the south-west (see 63, pages

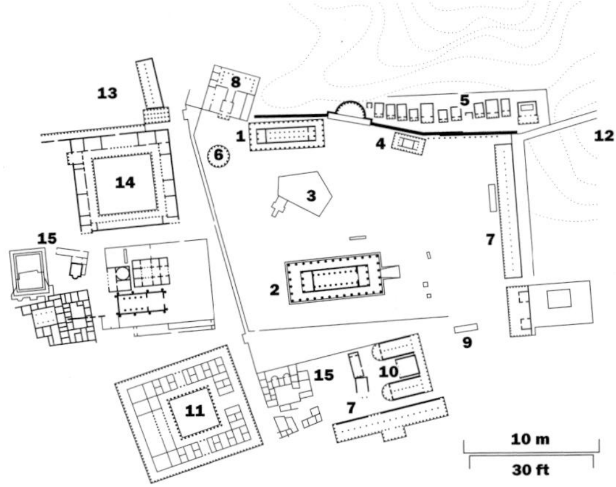

65 **Olympia, sanctuary of Zeus** plan of the reconstructed site.

(1) Heraeum (Temple of Hera); (2) Temple of Zeus; (3) central altar of Zeus; (4) Metroum (late-classical building dedicated to the mother of the gods) – there were 69 other altars and shrines on the site; (5) treasuries (mostly

consisting of simple rectangular cellas with porticos distyle in antis); (6) Philippeum, erected as a dynastic shrine by Philip II and Alexander the Great – there were many other monuments to past victors and donors, usually columns or pedestals supporting statues or trophies; (7) colonnades (stoas) protecting promenades and stalls selling everything from 'devotional requisites' to food and drink; (8) state dining halls (prytaneia); (9) main entrance to the sacred enclosure (given the form of a triumphal arch in the Roman imperial period, but originally probably a double portico of the Mycenaean type like the earliest-known sanctuary portals, c. 600 BC, at Samos and Aegina which incorporated stoas for the shelter of pilgrims); (10) council chamber (bouleterion) for the authorities charged with maintaining the site and organising the Games (consisting of two early archaic apsidal megarons with central colonnades – the northern one dating from the mid 6th century BC, the southern one earlier but rebuilt a century later – with a connecting colonnade and court added in the 4th century BC); (11) leonidaeum (with Ionic porticos and Doric court), a hostel for pilgrims or attendants at the Games; (12) the oldest Hellenic stadium for races (built into embankments in the absence of a natural hill to support the seats on either side of the

66 **Olympia, sanctuary of Zeus** view towards the ruins of the palaestra.

183-metre – 600-foot – track); (13) gymnasium for athletics (traditionally open, but framed with porticos and given a monumental gate in late-classical times); (14) palaestra for wrestling (always enclosed, but in late-classical times given a Doric peristyle before separate spaces for different age groups); (15) baths, with a cold-water washroom and separate cubicles – their close association with the palaestra provided a precedent for Roman development.

148–49) will reveal that the large simple mass of the Parthenon, with its extended horizontals and contracted verticals, was complemented by the disposition of the smaller, more complex masses of the Erechtheum and Propylaea to the other side of the centre of gravity established by the Parthenon's west front.

The Acropolis model and plan (see 48, pages 116–17) illustrate another crucial aspect of Greek site organisation. Framed by the central intercolumniation of the inner portico of the Propylaea, the visitor would have seen the cult statue of Athena just to the left of centre. Its base is perpendicular to the line of sight but not parallel with the wall behind it and the deflection points to the corners of that wall. A straight line drawn from our visitor's viewpoint to the right-hand corner may be extended to the central intercolumniation of the Parthenon's portico. A straight line similarly drawn in the other direction will lead to the central intercolumniation of the Erechtheum's main portico – so sight lines from the point of arrival plot the two other most important points on the site. This informal way of relating elements in space respects their integrity as mirror-image symmetry would not have done.

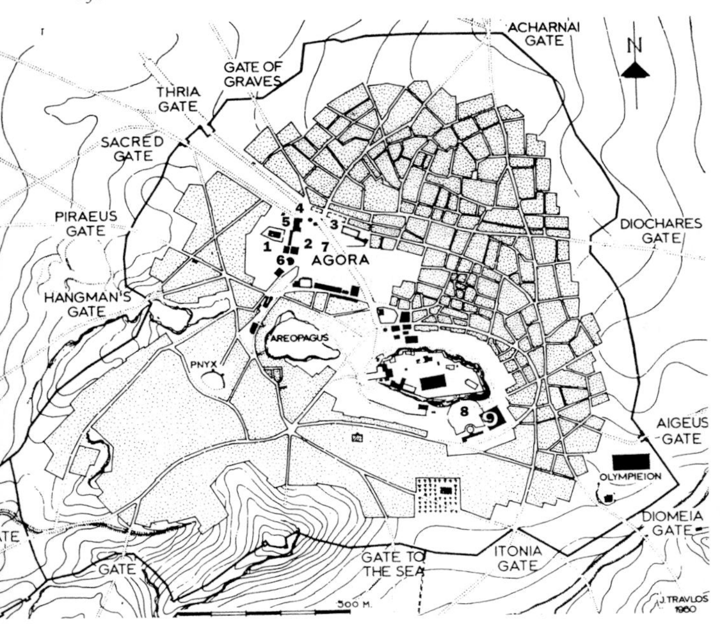
ACHARNAI GATE
N
GATE OF GRAVES
THRIA GATE
SACRED GATE
PIRAEUS GATE
DIOCHARES GATE
4
5
3
1
2
7
6
AGORA
HANGMAN'S GATE
AREOPAGUS
PNYX
8
AIGEUS GATE
OLYMPIEION
DIOMEIA GATE
TE
GATE
GATE TO THE SEA
ITONIA GATE
500 M.
J. TRAVLOS 1960

There is no sense of order in the areas around the social and commercial centre of ancient Athens, the agora.[67–68] These presumably followed the traditional growth pattern of towns before the intervention of planners, where feet tended to pick the easy way through the site contours, making the paths that became streets. Later, planners began to impose regular lines and to relate buildings to one another in accordance with clear geometrical patterns through the insertion of stoas.[69] Usually Doric with an internal Ionic colonnade supporting the ridge of the roof,

67 **Athens** plan of ancient town with agora.

(1) Hephaesteum; (2) new bouleterion (like its predecessor, this late 5th-century BC building was square with one side walled off to form an entrance lobby and seats for 700 around the other three sides, each c. 23 metres – 75 feet – long); (3) Poikile ('painted') Stoa; (4) Basileios ('royal') Stoa; (5) Zeus-Eleutherius Stoa, late 5th century BC; (6) tholos, c. 470 BC, the official dining hall of the Athenian senate (this was a walled rotunda 18.3 metres – 60 feet – in diameter with a conical roof supported by six internal columns); (7) site of original theatre; (8) Theatre of Dionysius; (9) odeon.

68 **Athens, agora** view from the west towards the Acropolis, showing the rebuilt Stoa of Attalus, left.

these were extended porticos for promenading and informal gatherings, often subdivided along the back into shops.

The imposition of formality

The cities of Hellas generally grew organically, but formality was brought to bear on rebuilding after devastation by war or earthquake, and, especially, in the laying out of new towns in the colonies. Here a regular grid appears as early as the late 7th century BC, not only in urban areas but also in the countryside – as at Metapontum in southern Italy.[70] Grids

69 **Athens, agora, Stoa of Attalus** interior (as rebuilt by the American School).

Though dating from the mid 2nd century BC, this example of a stoa follows the form evolved at Athens, Olympia and other early Hellenic sites during the 5th century. Open to the front through a Doric colonnade and walled to the back, the space was divided into two aisles by a central row of Ionic columns supporting the ridge of the pitched roof. Sometimes of two storeys, stoas might simply provide shelter for social intercourse or they might precede shops.

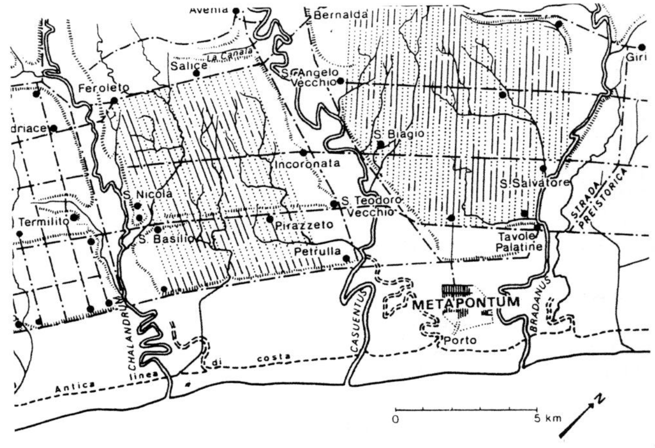

70 **Metapontum, southern Italy** plan showing the regular division of land in town and country.

Metapontum was laid out on the Gulf of Taranto in southern Italy towards the end of the 7th century BC. Surveys and sample excavation have revealed two phases of land division: with orthogonal tracks in the mid 6th century BC, then with a similar grid of drainage ditches less than a century later.

with broad arteries were also adopted for Paestum and Acragas. Naples and other southern Italian towns conformed to type later. Precedents were provided by the Babylonians and Egyptians: the great chronicler Herodotus knew about the regular division of the land in Egypt (see volume I, ORIGINS, page 152) and believed the Greeks learned the principles of land surveying from the Egyptians.

Miletus

The most celebrated exercise in Hellenic town planning was the rebuilding of Ionian Miletus – associated with the name of Hippodamus – in the generation following its destruction by the Persians in 494 BC. Hippodamus was a local physician, and the healthy circulation of air was a concern of his time. Far more rigid than his known work elsewhere, here a grid of nearly square blocks was imposed on the rugged promontory to either side of the harbour[71–72] – man asserting himself arrogantly over nature.

The redevelopment of Miletus was important not only because of its use of a grid to organise domestic quarters, but also because of its exploitation of the contours of the site to define different aspects of the

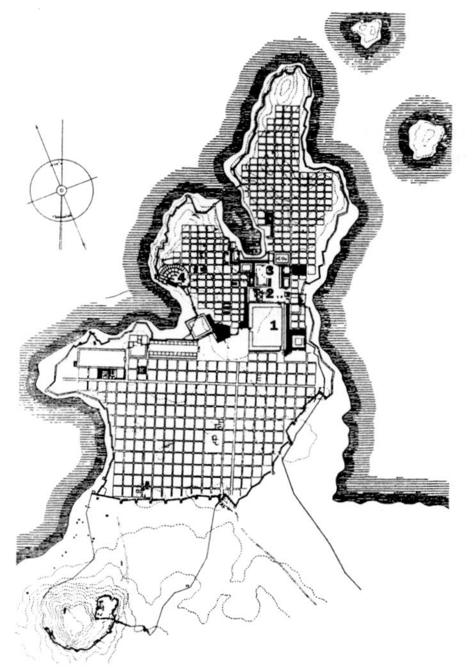
1
2
3
4

71 **Miletus, Ionia** plan of the city as rebuilt in the second quarter of the 5th century BC.

In the northern sector, where redevelopment began, the blocks of c. 23.8 by 29.3 metres (78 by 96 feet) were defined by streets c. 3.7 metres (12 feet) wide, except for one lateral artery running west from the central complex of public buildings. The southern sector was divided by two main arteries running north–south and east–west. These were c. 7.6 metres (25 feet) wide, the other streets were c. 4.3 metres (14 feet) wide and the blocks were 35.7 by 42.1 metres (117 by 138 feet).

(1) South agora, the main civic space, originally with stoas to the north, south and west sides and finally enclosed with the eastern stoa in the Hellenistic period; (2) Hellenistic bouleterion, built under Antiochus IV (175–164 BC) – beyond an open court, surrounded by Doric colonnades and containing an altar, the chamber itself, with its theatrical arrangement of seats, was covered by a truss roof supported by the walls and four Ionic columns; (3) north agora, enclosed and extended to the west with stoas forming subsidiary squares in the Hellenistic period; (4) Roman theatre.

72 **Miletus** view of site to the north from the Roman theatre.

Hippodamus, a local physician, is credited by Aristotle with the ordered rebuilding of Piraeus (towards the middle of the 5th century BC), and ancient sources also associate him with the founding of the colony of Thurii in southern Italy (444 BC). However, there is no evidence that he produced the exceptionally repetitive scheme for his native town.

city's life and different classes of housing. In the low ground beyond the harbour, towards the centre, public space and civic buildings separated the residential quarters from the commercial districts. The agoras, if more formally arranged than before, were not axially aligned – the formal relationship between buildings was doubtless the work of later ages. With its special emphasis on zoning, which appealed to Aristotle, the formula applied to Miletus may well have been drawn from Ionian precedents for orthogonal planning such as the early 7th-century rebuilding of Smyrna, if not from the western colonies.

The house plan

Regularisation was more supple on the mainland at Olynthus, where a new suburb was laid out c. 430 BC.[73] The grid of differentiated streets defines rectangular blocks, each containing ten square domestic plots. In accordance with timeless tradition in the lands to the east of the Mediterranean where civilisation developed, the houses turned largely blind fronts to the public domain and were oriented to the enclosed court which provided the main living space.[74] Entrance was invariably off-centre so that the main

0 50 100 m

part of the court could not be seen from the street. There was usually a portico on the northern side, facing south before the main room (oecus) which contained the hearth – as in the ancient megaron (see volume 1, ORIGINS, page 205). There was also usually a separate dining room (andron) for the master of the house and his friends. All these features were already present in Athenian houses built several generations earlier on more irregular sites.[75]

Sensitivity to site

Sensitivity to the natural landscape was the norm in the golden age of Hellenic classicism. This is nowhere better illustrated than at the Sicilian site of Segesta. Consummate in its discretion, the Temple of Athena here is set into a naturally beautiful place, comple-

73 **Olynthus, northern Greece** plan of the suburban extension laid out in the last quarter of the 5th century BC.

The main axes ran north–south, secondary streets east–west and the blocks were divided by alleys – also running east–west – into the two rows of plots c. 17 metres (56 feet) square on which the south-facing courtyard houses were built.

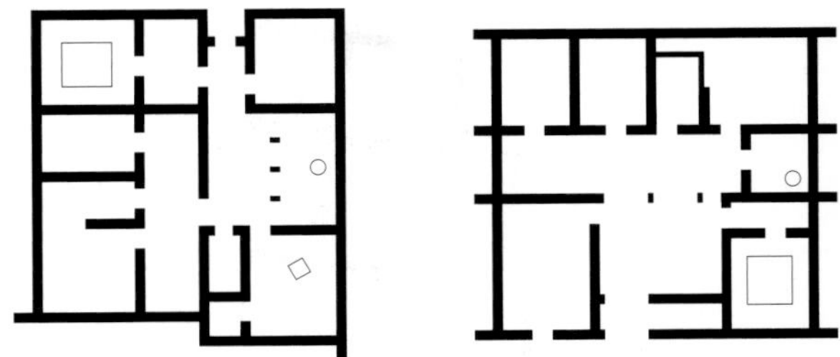

74 **Olynthus, house plans** late 5th century BC.

The off-centre entrance to each house was from the north or south, according to the situation of its plot in the block. In the former case (LEFT), the main suite of rooms separated the court from the street but was breached by a corridor; in the latter, only a vestibule screened the entrance. Sometimes the northern portico was extended all around the court as a peristyle.

Lit from two sides on a corner, the andron (dining room for the master of the house and his friends) was surrounded by couches for the diners raised above a central trough from which scraps could be flushed out into the adjacent street.

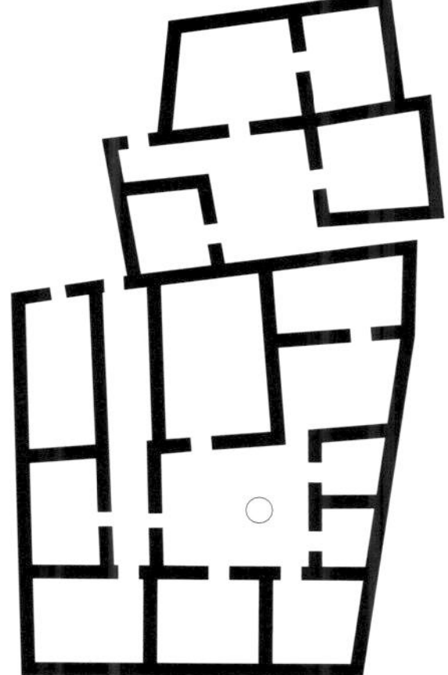

75 **Athens, house plan** early 5th century BC.

From the early archaic period onwards, the typical house had a court entered from a corner with rooms to three sides. In Athens spacious houses were rare, except in the suburbs, but two storeys were not uncommon.

76 **Segesta, Sicily, Temple, probably dedicated to Athena** c. 420 BC, view from the south-east.

On a stylobate 23.1 by 58 metres (75 feet 10 inches by 190 feet 5 inches) – a ratio of 1:2.51 – were six by 14 columns 1.96 by 9.37 metres (6 feet 5 inches by 30 feet 9 inches) throughout, giving proportions of 1:4.79. Intercolumniations were also uniform throughout, except for contraction at the corners. Begun while the city was

77 **Segesta, theatre** late 5th century BC.
The theatre well represents the stage of development reached in Athens a generation earlier.

allied with Athens after 426 BC, the temple was apparently left incomplete – with unfluted columns and no interior structure – after the defeat of Athens by Syracuse in 413 BC and the subsequent intervention of the Carthaginians.

menting and not compromising it.[76] The same is true of the theatre:[77] the simple semi-circular rings of seats are accommodated by a natural curve in the hillside, and over the low stage beyond the orchestra – as a backdrop to the action taking place – is a particularly beautiful view, itself part of the unfolding drama. As in the conception of the temple, an imposed rationalism – the pure geometry of a mind that sees in it the key to understanding the order of creation – complements the beauty of this world, imperfect though that was thought to be as a reflection of the design of the gods.

Building technology

Supported by terraced ground, the Greek theatre required no advanced building technology – the Greeks were concerned with refining their trabeated system, not with technological innovation. Having rejected irregularity towards the end of the archaic period, they developed masonry of great precision for walls as well as for columns. Large polygonal blocks subsisted in fortifications, but otherwise rectangular blocks were laid in regular courses – though concealed surfaces were often roughly cut for divergence, and

78 **Paestum, southern Italy, east gate** 5th century BC, inner face.

The Greek colonists of southern Italy seem to have been less prejudiced against the arch than their metropolitan contemporaries. Not uncommon for utilitarian works in Hellas (such as drains), the arch was used in city gates in Magna Graecia from at least the 6th century BC – as at Velia, another Greek colony to the south of Paestum.

outer faces were sometimes left coarse (rusticated) for greater apparent strength. Stability depended on dead weight, but in the most important buildings the blocks were secured to one another with dowels and clamps of iron or bronze rather than with mortar.

The Hellenes knew of the arch but were predisposed to the aesthetics of trabeation, usually bridging openings with a lintel or corbels. Applying oriental building technology to the construction of arched gates in their city walls from at least as early as the late 6th century BC,[78] however, the colonists of Magna Graecia left a major legacy to the Etruscans and Romans (see volume 3, IMPERIAL FORM).

the peloponnesian war and its aftermath

The houses of Olynthus and the Temple of Athena at Segesta bring us to the period in which Hellas was destroying itself in the Peloponnesian War (431–404 BC). The war, between a league of Dorians led by the Spartans and a largely Ionian league led by the Athenians, placed in opposition those very traits which had fused to take Hellenic culture to its summit – Doric virility and strength, but rigidity; Ionic grace and vitality, but capriciousness – and destroyed the very institution upon which that unique achievement depended: the polis. The complexity of the war and its causes, and the complexity of warfare itself, promoted the professional specialist and, therefore, the individual, whereas the polis depended on all its citizens being good, if essentially amateur, 'all-rounders'. Now all the Hellenes were exhausted, and the confidence of all but the Spartans in their institutions was undermined.

The Spartans triumphed, briefly – partly through the invincibility of their army, but more through Persian aid and the folly of the Athenians in squandering their sea power on extraneous adventures, most lamentably in Sicily. Persia was the real victor, however, and the price for the intervention of its 'Great King' was Ionia. Elsewhere Spartan 'protection' – exercised through the imposition of oligarchies on the defeated democracies – soon excited reaction.

A renewal of war ended in 387 BC with the mediation of the 'Great King' as the guarantor of autonomy among the constituents of Hellas. Thebes challenged Sparta in leadership and astonished everyone by defeating the Spartan army in battle in 371. But Thebes was not capable of sustained dominance, and the rude northern kingdom of Macedon was the ultimate beneficiary with the accession of the wily Philip II in 359: he imposed his own peace with garrisons. On his early death, his extraordinary son, Alexander the Great, not only sustained Macedonian dominance in Hellas but led the Hellenes to overrun the empire of the Persians, which by then extended over most of the world known to them. Alexander died in 323 BC at the age of 33 – but that world was changed forever.

Platonic Rationalism

Contemptuous of the disastrous factional amateurism of Athenian democracy, the great philosopher Plato sought the ideal alternative in the name of his master Socrates (470–399 BC) – who had himself perished at the hands of Athenian democrats. The vast scope of Plato's teaching in the academy he established in Athens early in the 380s BC goes way beyond our concern, but his Rationalism is of fundamental importance to all aspects of classical culture, not least architecture.

In the disillusioned Athens of the period following the severe reverses of the Peloponnesian War, the sceptical teachers known as Sophists challenged the old puritan values in a spirit of pragmatic humanism. Protagoras in particular denied that there were absolute standards and objective truths, with the contention that: 'man is the measure of all things, of things that are that they are, and of things that are not that they are not.' Precisely because man is the arbiter, in practice in society the majority must prevail with the customs and conventions accepted by that majority.

Didactic in purpose, predisposed to belief in the absolute Good, Plato pits his master against the Sophists on ground that is at once Rationalist and mystical. If he acquired his ethical bias from Socrates, it was from the greatest of the pre-Socratic philosophers, Parmenides and Heracleitus respectively, that Plato extracted the positive and negative ideas that all being was eternal, homogeneous and logically unsusceptible to change, and that there is nothing stable in the sensible world. The combination led back to Pythagoras and Orphic mysticism.

To Plato, the philosopher is a lover of the vision of Truth; it is difficult entirely to disassociate the vision from the mystical or the love from the ecstasy of the mystics. Apprehension of Truth alone is knowledge, and that is to be gained not from experience but through deductive reasoning from self-evident axioms such as mathematics: it is not empirical (*a posteriori*) but rational (*a priori*). Knowledge is of universals, the ultimate Realities which Plato identifies as Ideas or Forms made by God. Reason will lead the soul to their vision. Sense perception, on the other hand, informs only opinion, for it is attuned to the particulars of this ever-changing, contradictory world – beautiful things, for instance, may also be ugly, as distinct from Beauty itself, which is immutable. Moreover, if this world is perverted by 'irrational necessity', Plato held it as self-evident that Reality, as opposed to appearance, is completely good. Thus if the ideal is intellectual, like the Pythagorean Good, it is also mystical: knowledge is the revelation of the divine.

The Platonic theory of Forms

Qualified in Pythagorean terms of Number, Plato's theory of Forms provides the basis for his explanation of the cosmos. Returning to mythology in arguing against chance, Plato postulates the rational and therefore comprehensible purpose of a creator: Soul. Like elemental Mind, Soul is also like – but not called – Zeus. He presides over a hierarchy of powers but is (unfortunately) not omnipotent as Craftsman. His reason is not sovereign over the irrational force of physical necessity, since the material he has to use (evidently pre-existent) will not be consistent in all its properties with the faithful reproduction of his Model. That is the world of Being, the true world of Forms, the Good; the product is the world of Becoming, our imperfect world.

In pursuit of perfection, Soul builds by introducing mathematical form and harmony to the conditions of chaos, first defining the four basic elements and then relating them in constant proportions. These elements are the four regular solids constituted from the most elementary of plane figures, the triangle. They are the tetrahedron (fire), octahedron (air) and icosahedron (water), all generated from the isosceles halves of the square, and the cube (earth), generated from the scalene halves of the equilateral triangle.[79] Though not similarly generated from triangles, the dodecahedron is added to represent the universe, which is otherwise defined as spherical because 'like is fairer than unlike and only a sphere is alike in all aspects'.

The concept of a supersensory world of eternal ideals, inherently discounting the material world of appearances, was to be perennially attractive – most notably, perhaps, as the New Jerusalem of Christ. Yet Plato's attempt to deal with the idea of the universal through his theory of Forms was far from completely resolved – especially for material things and negatives, let alone the problem of relating Reality's timelessness to its creation. His pupil, Aristotle, was to reject it.

79 **Platonic solids.**

(1) Square divided on its diagonal into isosceles triangles; (2) equilateral triangle divided into scalene triangles; (3) cube; (4) tetrahedron; (5) octahedron; (6) icosahedron; (7) dodecahedron.

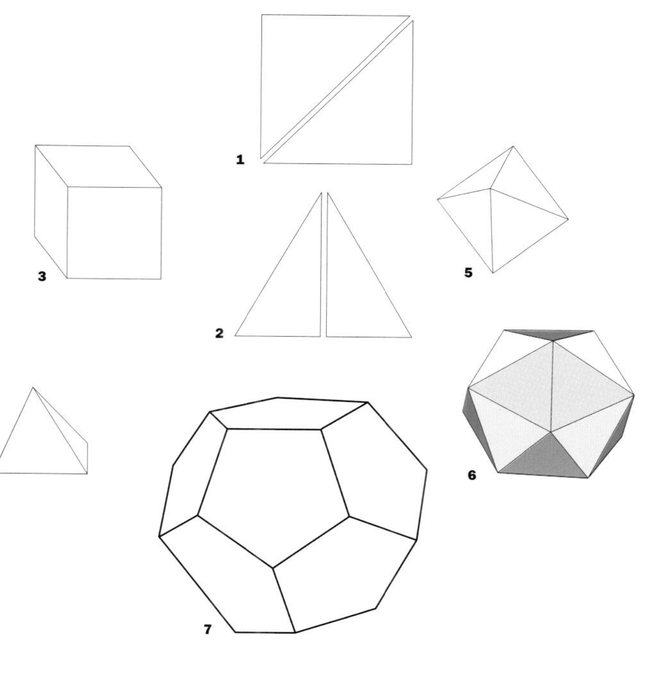
1
3
5
2
6
7

Aristotelian empiricism

Aristotle (who was tutor to Alexander the Great, without notable effect) agreed that philosophers must seek objective truth in the knowledge of immaterial and unchanging universals, but he promoted argument from verifiable premises as well as from abstract hypotheses like those of mathematics – inductive as well as deductive reasoning. Totally detached from the experience of this world, the first principles on which Plato's deduction depends are articles of faith to which Aristotle could not subscribe. And he found in Plato's conception no convincing explanation of the concrete individual things of our experience, which he saw as the primary realities. To Aristotle, universals were not transcendent, but were immanent in the general characteristics of the particular things we perceive. Hence it was to this changeable world that he looked for the unchangeable objects of true knowledge, not beyond it.

Plato, of course, looked for unchangeable Reality elsewhere precisely because he could not identify it in a world of apparent change. In abandoning that position, Aristotle had to account for unchangeable Reality and the reality of change. He distinguished form, matter and substance, potentiality and actuality. Substance is matter defined by a particular form; form is potential in raw matter, actual in substance moulded by evolution. By definition, specific substances lose their identity in change, but beyond them Aristotle saw evolution progressing to ever greater actuality: its objective is the perfect form and unchangeable actuality of God. As Bertrand Russell put it: Plato was mathematical, Aristotle was biological – he was, in fact, the first empirical biologist.

Though the philosophy of his predecessors was mainly Rationalist, Aristotle's empiricism was hardly revolutionary. He sought a balance between the rational and the empirical: in his ethics it is as a mean between extremes that he defines virtue. Experience had naturally governed some lines of earlier Greek enquiry, notably medicine, and it is difficult to imagine that the Greek artist framed the anthropomorphic ideal of the gods without reference to himself and the people around him – seeking a mean between extreme examples, as we have seen.

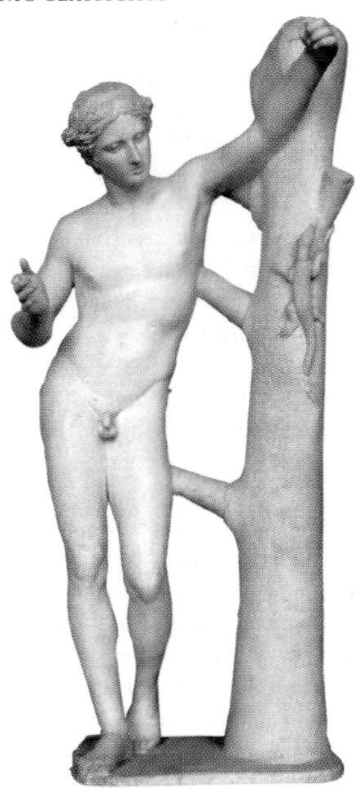

If the rationalist concept of the mean guided the development of classical art to its apogee towards the middle of the 5th century BC, empiricism accompanied by loss of faith in old reason produced a very different art in the first half of the 4th century BC. Just when the Dorians triumphed in war, the Ionians triumphed in art. In both sculpture and architecture, the Doric canon succumbed to Phidias' and Ictinus' introduction of lighter, more graceful Ionic attitudes.

Compare Praxiteles – perhaps the most significant sculptor in the generation after Phidias – with Polycleitus. Dating from c. 390 BC, Praxiteles' statue is supposed to be the sun god Apollo[80] – also the patron of art and music – but has a distinctly female lightness, grace and elegance. So lacking is it in virility, in fact, that it can no longer support itself – in contrast with the discretion of Polycleitus' original bronze (see 41, page 99). The emasculation also reflects Ionic sensuality: Praxiteles' marble now has the softness of flesh rather than the hardness of muscle, and the softness of the modelling is enhanced by the modulation of the light.

A major achievement of Praxiteles was to abandon

80 **Praxiteles: Apollo** c. 390 BC.

the fixed frontal viewpoint and compose in the round. This statue belongs to our space. Interest in human space and traits informed Praxiteles' work. His was an essentially realistic response to the emotional and physical realities of this world, a representation of figures less as abstract ideals than as human.

These developments should be seen against the background of the trauma of the Peloponnesian War: the interest in the real, the human, the sensual and the emotional may be traced to the collapse of the old austere ideals that devalued the realities of this world in the certainty of Order in creation as a whole. What these statues reveal foreshadows what was to happen in architecture.

The Temple of Apollo Epicurius at Bassae

The next important work after the completion of the Parthenon was the Temple of Apollo Epicurius at Bassae in the Peloponnesus,[81–82] attributed to Ictinus. The columns of its Doric pteron approach the proportions of the Parthenon, but the architect furthered the eclecticism of the great Athenian work, replacing superimposed Doric Orders with an inverted Ionic pteron in the cella and elaborating the capital of the central col-

81 **Bassae, Temple of Apollo Epicurius** last quarter of the 5th century BC.

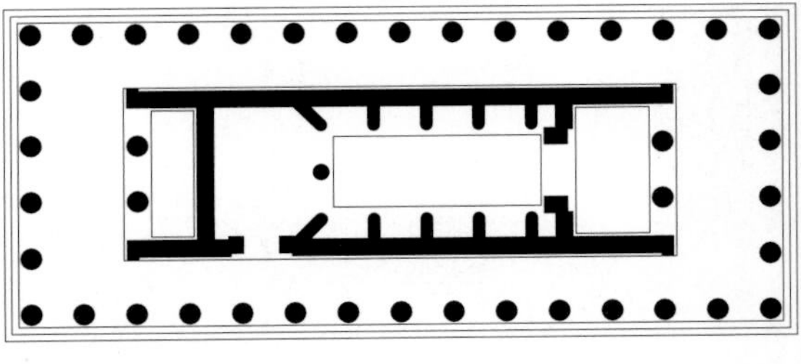

82 **Bassae, Temple of Apollo Epicurius** plan and reconstructed view of the interior.

On a stylobate 14.5 by 38.2 metres (47 feet 6 inches by 125 feet 5 inches) – a ratio of 1:2.64 – were six by 15 columns 1.17 to 1.12 by 5.96 metres (3 feet 10 inches to 3 feet 8 inches by 19 feet 6½ inches), giving proportions of 1:5.13 on the front and 1:5.31 on the sides. The axial spacing was 2.71 metres (8 feet 10¾ inches) on the front – a ratio of 2.34:1 and 1:2.19 to base diameter and column height respectively – and slightly narrower on the sides.

Pausanias attributes the temple to Ictinus and ascribes

the dedication to gratitude for relief from the plague. The outstanding novelty of the design – the attached Order of Ionic and proto-Corinthian columns supporting the magnificent high-relief frieze within the cella – contrasts with the archaic proportions of the plan, which may be explained by the wish of the remote provincial patrons to acknowledge the precedent of the great Temple of Apollo at Delphi (see 38, pages 88–89). The Order was modern in its proportions and the steep slope of the echinus, but the patrons seem also to have had their archaic way in the three incised rings at the top of the column. The provincial builders, moreover, were apparently not called upon to cope with sophisticated optical-illusion controls such as the curvature of stylobate and entablature, though the columns have slight entasis.

The Order within is peculiar, not only in the introduction of the Corinthian capital but also in the form of the Ionic, with volutes to all three exposed sides and bell-shaped bases. No special provision seems to have been made for lighting the battles between Greeks and Amazons and Lapiths and Centaurs in the magnificent frieze.

umn opposite the entrance with acanthus leaves in the way later to be identified as Corinthian. That column apart, the internal supports are attached to short spur walls: like Praxiteles' Apollo, they are no longer virile, self-supporting entities.

Before Bassae, the Doric temple had been primarily an object of external formal perfection. It was not a congregational building: the priests performed rites within; the public participated in worship outside. Bassae's architect, however, took a revolutionary interest in the embellishment of interior space.

The column as decoration

Two superb little round buildings from early in the 4th century BC (tholoi) continue the line of development pursued at Bassae, producing an increasing visual richness at the expense of strength and self-reliance. The older one, in the sanctuary of Athena Pronaea at Delphi,[83–84] is Doric outside but has an inner ring of proto-Corinthian columns attached to the cella wall. The tholos in the sanctuary of Asclepius at Epidaurus[85–86] is also Doric outside, but inside a ring of free-standing Corinthian columns achieves the same height on a much narrower base.

83 **Delphi, tholos in the sanctuary of Athena Pronaea** early 4th century BC, view of the ruins from the north.

84 **Delphi, tholos in the sanctuary of Athena Pronaea** reconstructed elevation and part section.

Attributed to Theodorus of Phocaea, who wrote a treatise on it, the marble rotunda – 13.5 metres (44 feet 3 inches) in diameter – consisted of a circular cella surrounded by a ring of 20 Doric columns outside and 9 attached

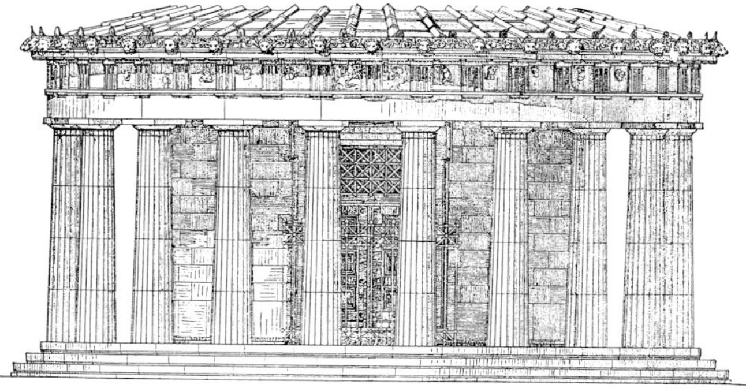

Corinthian half-columns on a raised ledge inside (the door occupied the place of the tenth). The Doric Order probably matched that of the Temple of Apollo Epicurius at Bassae, unlike the modern reconstruction, which is almost certainly anachronistically elongated at 1:8.46.

The remains of an archaic precedent for this type of circular building were discovered in the main precinct at Delphi. Of limestone, this had an outer ring of 13 Doric columns, to which the 20 metopes and their defining triglyphs in the frieze were evidently entirely unrelated.

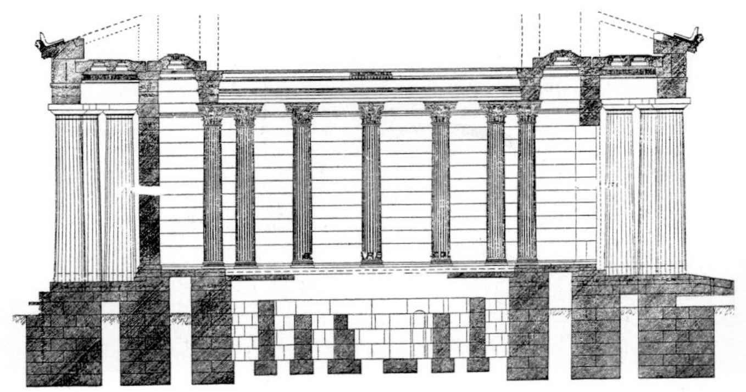

85 **Epidaurus, tholos in the sanctuary of Asclepius** c. 360 BC, section and plan.

Attributed to Polycleitus the Younger by Pausanias, this was built of tufa without and marble within. On a stylobate 21.3 metres (69 feet 10 inches) in diameter, the circular cella was ringed by 26 Doric columns outside and 14 freestanding Corinthian columns inside.

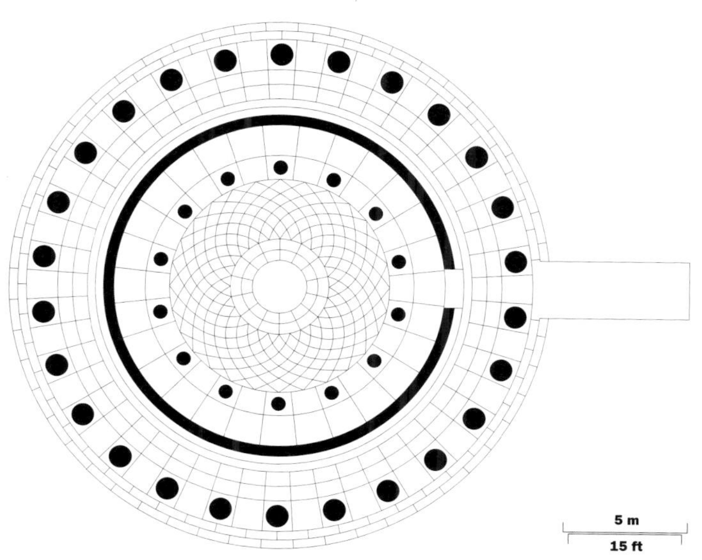
5 m
15 ft

The column had been the main agent of support before Bassae; now it was reduced to the decorative role of articulating the forces implicit in the exercise. Fostering ambiguity between appearance and reality, this development was far advanced by the middle of the 4th century BC in the Temple of Athena Alea at Tegea[87] and the Temple of Zeus at Nemea.[89] In both, the proportions of the external Doric Order approximated the Ionic: virility ceded to effeminacy. In both the Corinthian interior approached maturity:[88] structural logic ceded to ornament. At Nemea the internal colonnade was freestanding, as at Epidaurus. At Tegea it was attached, as at Delphi, but on a much more significant scale it marks the abrogation of the logic on which classical lucidity was based. The very ambiguity of the situation in which column and wall are confused with one another, charging the space they enclose with tension, elicits an emotional response against the appeal of reason.

86 **Epidaurus, tholos in the sanctuary of Asclepius** detail of surviving fragments of external and internal Orders (Epidaurus Museum).

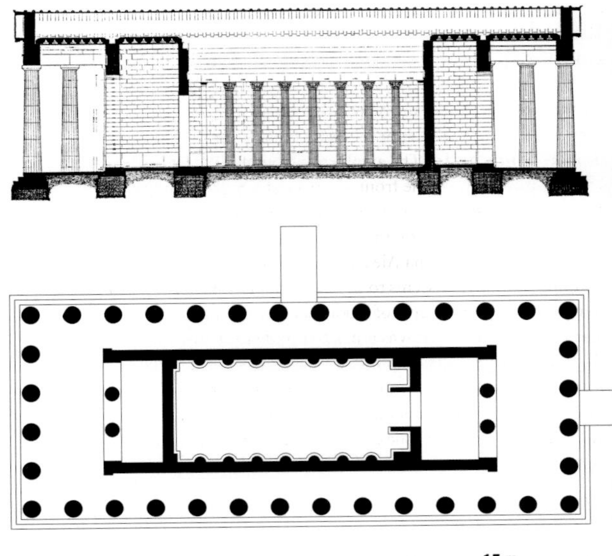
15 m
45 ft

87 **Tegea, Temple of Athena Alea** c. 350 BC (built in place of an archaic building destroyed by fire in 394 BC), section and plan.

On a stylobate 19.2 by 47.5 metres (63 by 156 feet) – a ratio of 1:2.48 – were six by 14 columns 1.55 by 9.47 metres (5 feet 1 inch by 31 feet 1 inch), giving proportions of 1:6.11. The axial spacing was 3.61 metres (11 feet 10 inches) on the front – a ratio of 2.33:1 and 1:2.62 to base diameter and column height respectively – and minutely narrower on the sides.

The Temple of Athena Alea at Tegea is attributed to the sculptor Scopas, and seems to have been commissioned to rival the nearby Temple of Apollo Epicurius at Bassae (see 81–82, pages 191–93). It was typical of its time in its slender Doric proportions and combination of Orders, but not in its retention of an opisthodomos, or the extension of its sides to 14 columns to contain the opisthodomos and accommodate a door to the cella in the centre of the northern side.

88 **The development of the Corinthian capital.**

(1) Bassae, Temple of Apollo Epicurius: engraving of the fragment of the proto-Corinthian capital found during the excavations of 1812 but now lost, and restored sketch. The designer – identified as Callimachus of Corinth by Vitruvius – returned to the Egyptian lotus motif of the proto-Ionic (see 17, page 52), combined it with the Mesopotamian palmette, and added two rows of 20 small acanthus leaves in alternation above the concave recessions and raised edges of the flutes of the column.

(2) Delphi, tholos in the sanctuary of Athena Pronaea: restoration from excavated fragments of the proto-Corinthian capitals attached to the interior of the rotunda. This permutation recalls the Order of the Temple of Apollo Epicurius at Bassae (1), except that the central tendrils are united with the corner ones in an 's' scroll.

(3) Epidaurus, tholos in the sanctuary of Asclepius: engraving of a model capital buried at the time of construction and recovered intact. In essence, the architect Polycleitus the Younger achieved the canonical form of the Corinthian capital here. No longer alternating in two small bands, the acanthus leaves rise to more than half the height of the bell and the tendrils spring up from behind them; there are flowers in the centre of each side.

(4) Tegea, Temple of Athena Alea: engraved restoration from excavated remains of the capitals of the half-columns attached to the cella walls. The form is related in general to the Epidauran model (3), with generous acanthus foliage, but the proportions are squatter, the spiral tendrils supporting the corners of the abacus are sheathed with partially open leaves (caulicoli), and there is another leaf instead of the central spirals.

(5) Athens, Temple of Olympian Zeus, c. 170 BC: engraving of mature Corinthian capital.

89 **Nemea, Temple of Zeus** c. 340 BC, view of the ruins from the south.

On a stylobate 20 by 42.6 metres (65 feet 11 inches by 139 feet 8 inches) – a ratio of 1:2.12 – the six by 12 Doric columns were 1.63 by 10.36 metres (5 feet 4 inches by 34 feet), giving proportions of 1:6.35. The axial spacing was 3.75 metres (12 feet 3 3/4 inches) on the front – a ratio of 2.29:1 and 1:2.76 to base diameter and column height respectively – and minutely narrower on the sides. Typical of late classical practice in dispensing with an opisthodomos, the plan retained a sunken adytum, which was screened from the cella, as at the Temple of Apollo Epicurius at Bassae (see 82, page 192). Most unusually, the Corinthian Order was surmounted by the Ionic.

The Hellenistic period

The appeal to emotion rather than reason through the manipulation of form and scale, and the promotion of oriental splendour, were major motives behind the evolution of art in the so-called Hellenistic period which followed Alexander the Great's conquest of Persia in 330 BC. These brought forth the style later to be called baroque. Equally characteristic of the period were mannerist virtuosity of invention in ornament and the wilful flouting of convention – hence expectation – in mixing the elements of the Orders and, above all, in confusing the roles of column and wall by denying the independent virility of the former and reducing it to a mere agent articulating the forces implicit in the latter. Mannerism was to prove perennially popular at royal courts; baroque well served the super-state.

Long before the accession of Alexander, even before Dorian logic and lucidity were being flouted at Tegea, a new dimension of lavishness celebrated the self-inflicted ruin of the polis. This had always been to the taste of the more sensual Ionians. Now it was manifest first in honour of the Persian king at Sardis,[90] then in the elevation of his servants, such as Mausolus of Halicarnassus.[91] Beyond the central importance man had always had in Hellenic culture, men now asserted their own importance as kings in a way which the earlier Hellenes had rejected. Of course, the Hellenes had conceived their gods in ideal human terms, occasionally representing them as overwhelming in size – as with Zeus at Olympia (see 4, page 15) or Athena on the Athenian Acropolis – but the assertion of the superiority of an individual man over other men had not

90 **Sardis, Temple of Artemis-Cybele** begun c. 360 BC (in place of its predecessor, destroyed in 497), but left unfinished.

On a stylobate 45.7 by 99 metres (150 by 325 feet) – a ratio of 1:2.17 – was an outer pteron of eight by 20 columns, on average 1.9 by 17.73 metres (6 feet 3 inches by 58 feet 2 inches), giving proportions of 1:9.31. Within the pteron, both pronaos and opisthodomos were given prostyle tetrastyle porticos. The cella floor was raised above the level of the pronaos. The opisthodomos opened into a vestibule, beyond which was an adytum.

The largest columns erected in their time, those of the outer pteron had plinths and bases of scotia and torus mouldings conforming to the Ionian norm but with varied embellishment to the torus. Most of them were never fluted.

Two each of the pronaos and opisthodomos columns were smaller than the rest since they stood on square pedestals which were apparently meant to be sculpted in emulation of the embellishment to the lower drums of the columns at the Artemisium in Ephesus (see 25, page 66). The capitals were embellished with acanthus scrolls or the Mesopotamian palmette in concession to Persian taste (as Dinsmoor plausibly speculates).

been a theme of Hellenic art. Colossal building was uncommon too, except occasionally in the colonies and in Asia Minor, where oriental magnificence had always been an inspiration. With the eclipse of the polis – and the emasculation of the Doric Order – the Dorian had had its day, and the Hellenistic age of the Macedonian was to issue from the cross-fertilisation of the Ionian and the Persian.

91 **Statue of Mausolus of Halicarnassus** satrap of Caria, from his mausoleum (London, British Museum).

glossary

ABACUS flat slab forming the top of a CAPITAL. (See page 42.)

ACROPOLIS highest part or citadel of a city, usually the area containing the principal public buildings. (See page 117.)

ACROTERIUM ornamental finial, usually supported on a PLINTH, at the apex or side of a PEDIMENT. (See page 42.)

ADYTUM inner sanctum of a temple.

AGORA open space used as a marketplace or assembly area. (See pages 160–61.)

AISLE side passage of a temple, running parallel to the NAVE and separated from it by COLUMNS or PIERS.

ANDRON dining room in a private house, reserved for the use of the master of the household and his male guests. (See page 172.)

ANNULET small flat ring around the SHAFT of a COLUMN.

ANTA a PILASTER at the end of a side wall between two of which one or more COLUMNS may be placed, which are then IN ANTIS.

ANTEFIXES blocks used as ornaments in, for instance, a CORNICE to conceal the ends of tiles.

ANTHEMION ornament in the form of a continuous pattern of alternate palmettes and lotus flowers connected by scrolls. (See page 53.)

APSE semi-circular domed or vaulted space, especially at one end of a BASILICA. Hence apsidal, in the shape of an apse.

ARCHITRAVE one of the three principal elements of an ENTABLATURE, positioned immediately above the CAPITAL of a COLUMN, and supporting the FRIEZE and CORNICE. (See pages 42, 54.)

ASHLAR masonry cut and placed in horizontal courses with vertical joints, so as to present a smooth surface.

ASTRAGAL small moulding with circular or semi-circular cross-section.

ATLANTE element in the shape of a male figure, used in place of a COLUMN. (See pages 46, 48.)

BEAM horizontal element in, for instance, a TRABEATED structure.

BIT-HILANI columned PORTICO, specifically of 1st millennium BC Syria.

BLIND WALL wall without doors or windows.

BOULETERION meeting hall for formal gatherings of senators or councillors.

BRACKET CAPITAL load-bearing member projecting from a CAPITAL or forming a projecting CAPITAL, for instance an IONIC VOLUTE.

CAPITAL top part of a COLUMN, supporting the ENTABLATURE. The part of the COLUMN which, taken together with the ENTABLATURE, forms the major defining element in the Greek ORDERS of architecture – DORIC, IONIC and CORINTHIAN. (See pages 42, 52–54, 207.)

CARYATID female figure used as a support in place of a COLUMN. (See pages 57, 141.)

CAULICOLI carved plant stalks bearing the acanthus leaves supporting the VOLUTES of a CORINTHIAN CAPITAL. (See page 205.)

CAVETTO style of concave moulding with a quarter-circular cross-section.

CELLA the sanctuary of a temple, usually containing the cult statue.

CHRYSELEPHANTINE gold and ivory used together as overlay.

COLONNADE line of regularly spaced COLUMNS.

COLUMN vertical member, usually circular in cross-section, functionally structural or ornamental or both, comprising a base, SHAFT and CAPITAL. (See pages 42, 54.)

COLUMN IN ANTIS a COLUMN deployed in a PORTICO between ANTAE, as opposed to standing proud of the façade.

CONSOLE support bracket, ornamental in form, with a curved outline.

CORBEL course of masonry or support bracket, usually stone, for a BEAM or other horizontal member. Hence corbelled, forming a stepped roof from progressively overlapping corbels.

CORINTHIAN ORDER *see* ORDER, CORINTHIAN.

CORNICE projecting moulding forming the top part of an ENTABLATURE. (See pages 42, 54.)

CORONA projecting element in the upper part of a CORNICE with a flat vertical face and undercut with a concave SOFFIT to prevent water from running down the walls of a building. (See pages 42, 54.)

CREPIDOMA steps forming the platform of a Greek temple.

CYCLOPEAN MASONRY masonry made up of massive irregular blocks of undressed stone.

CYMA RECTA wave-shaped moulding, usually forming all or part of a CORNICE, the upper part convex and the lower concave. (See pages 42, 54.)

CYMA REVERSA wave-shaped moulding, usually forming all or part of a CORNICE, the upper part concave and the lower convex.

DADO the middle part, between base and CORNICE, of a PEDESTAL or the lower part of a wall when treated as a continuous pedestal.

DENTILS small blocks deployed in horizontal lines, typically forming part of the IONIC and CORINTHIAN CORNICES. (See page 54.)

DIPTERAL building with a double row of COLUMNS around it.

DISTYLE a PORTICO with two COLUMNS.

DISTYLE IN ANTIS inset PORTICO with two COLUMNS set between two PIERS.

DORIC ORDER *see* ORDER, DORIC.

DOWEL short rod of wood or metal used to join together two pieces of stone, as in the drums of COLUMNS.

ECHINUS quarter-round convex projection or moulding on a cushion supporting the ABACUS of the CAPITAL of a COLUMN. (See page 42.)

EGG-AND-DART MOULDING decoration on an OVOLO moulding consisting of alternating shapes of eggs and arrow-heads. (See page 54.)

ENTABLATURE part of the façade immediately above the COLUMNS, usually composed of a supportive ARCHITRAVE, decorative FRIEZE and projecting CORNICE. (See pages 42, 54.)

ENTASIS slight bulge in a COLUMN, designed to overcome the optical illusion of a straight column being slightly concave. (See page 128.)

EUTHYNTERIA top of the foundation of a building, levelled so as to present a usable platform on which to build.

FASCIA plain horizontal band, or the flat surfaces which together form an ARCHITRAVE.

FILLET top part of a CORNICE, or generally a decorative moulding in the shape of a narrow raised band.

FRIEZE the middle part of an ENTABLATURE, above the ARCHITRAVE and below the CORNICE, or more generally any horizontal strip decorated in RELIEF. (See pages 42, 56.)

GALLERY upper storey projecting over the main space.

GUTTAE projections, more or less conical in form, carved beneath the TRIGLYPHS of a DORIC ENTABLATURE. (See page 42.)

GYMNASIUM building or enclosed area for the performance of athletics.

HEXASTYLE a PORTICO with six COLUMNS.

HIGH RELIEF *see* RELIEF.

HIPPED ROOF *see* ROOF, HIPPED.

HYPETHRAL a temple with a wholly or partly unroofed NAOS.

IONIC ORDER *see* ORDER, IONIC.

JAMB side of a doorway or window frame.

JOISTS horizontal timbers supporting a floor.

KORE female figure carved in stone, usually clothed and freestanding. (See page 39.)

KOUROS male figure carved in stone, usually naked and freestanding. (See page 38.)

LANTERN open structure, admitting light and air, situated at a building's highest point.

LINTEL horizontal member over a window or doorway or bridging the gap between two COLUMNS or PIERS.

LOW RELIEF *see* RELIEF.

MEGARON rectangular hall forming the principal interior space of a palace.

METOPE originally the space between the TRIGLYPHS in a DORIC FRIEZE, and subsequently the panel, often carved in RELIEF, occupying that space. (See page 42.)

MUTULE projecting block above the TRIGLYPH of a DORIC ENTABLATURE. (See page 42.)

NAOS main chamber of a temple, usually housing the cult statue.

NAVE central body of principal interior of, for instance, a temple.

OCTASTYLE a PORTICO with eight COLUMNS.

ODEON roofed building for the performance of music.

OECUS principal room of a Greek private house.

OPISTHODOMOS porch or room at the rear of a temple, sometimes used as a treasury.

ORCHESTRA circular or semi-circular space in front of the stage of a theatre, where the chorus performed.

ORDER defining feature of classical architecture, comprising a COLUMN together with its ENTABLATURE.

ORDER, CORINTHIAN an evolution from the IONIC Order, characterised by the replacement of the CAPITAL VOLUTES with a more elaborate and deeper decorative arrangement. (See page 205.)

ORDER, DORIC the oldest and most simply functional of the three Greek Orders of architecture, characterised by a fluted and tapered COLUMN without a base, topped by a plain CAPITAL, surmounted by a relatively high ENTABLATURE. (See page 42.)

ORDER, IONIC slightly later and more elaborate Order than the DORIC, featuring fluted COLUMNS that have bases and are topped by CAPITALS with scrolled VOLUTES. The COLUMNS typically are taller relative to their base diameters than the DORIC, and are correspondingly less acutely tapered. The ENTABLATURE was less tall than the DORIC, being originally composed of ARCHITRAVE and CORNICE only, though a FRIEZE became usual later. (See page 54.)

OVOLO projecting convex moulding. (See page 46.)

PALAESTRA public building for training in athletics, typically smaller than a GYMNASIUM.

PALMETTE ornament reminiscent of a stylised palm-leaf. (See page 52.)

PARASCENIUM projecting wings extending from the SCENA to embrace the PROSCENIUM.

PEDESTAL base supporting a COLUMN or statue.

PEDIMENT triangular area of wall, usually a gable, above the ENTABLATURE. (See page 42.)

PERIPTERAL building whose main part is flanked by a single PERISTYLE.

PERISTYLE row of COLUMNS surrounding a building or courtyard, or a courtyard so COLONNADED.

PIER supporting pillar for a wall or roof, often of rectangular cross-section.

PILASTER a PIER of rectangular cross-section, more or less integral with and only slightly projecting from the wall which it supports.

PITCHED ROOF *see* ROOF, PITCHED.

PLINTH rectangular base or base support of a COLUMN or wall. (See page 54.)

PODIUM continuous base or PEDESTAL, consisting of PLINTH, DADO and CORNICE, supporting a series of COLUMNS; also a platform enclosing the arena of an amphitheatre.

PORTICO entrance to a building featuring a COLONNADE.

POST vertical element in, for instance, a TRABEATED structure.

POSTERN small gateway or door, usually at the back of a building.

PRONAOS area in front of the principal room of a temple (the NAOS), typically with walls to the sides and COLUMNS to the fore.

PROPYLAEUM gateway, especially to a temple enclosure.

PROSCENIUM stage on which the principal actors performed, in front of the SCENA and behind the ORCHESTRA.

PROSTYLE row of COLUMNS standing in front of a building, usually forming an open PORTICO.

PRYTANEION public hall for formal dining and entertaining.

PTERON a COLONNADE flanking a temple.

REGULA short band above the GUTTAE on a DORIC ENTABLATURE. (See page 42.)

RELIEF carving, typically of figures, raised from a flat background by cutting away more (HIGH RELIEF) or less (LOW RELIEF) of the material from which they are carved. (See page 124.)

ROOF, HIPPED roof composed of a PITCHED ROOF with inclined (as opposed to vertical) planes at the ends.

ROOF, PITCHED roof composed of two inclined planes whose point of contact forms the ridge or highest line. (See page 17.)

ROSETTE projecting or incised ornament in a wall or ceiling carved so as to resemble a rose.

SCENA structure in a theatre in front of which the principal actors performed, and behind or inside which off-stage action purported to take place.

SCOTIA concave moulding, usually on the base of a COLUMN, often between two convex TORUS mouldings and providing an apparently deep channel between them. (See page 54.)

SCREEN WALL false (non-structural) wall to the front of a building, masking the façade proper.

SHAFT more or less cylindrical element of a COLUMN rising from the base to the CAPITAL. (See pages 42, 54.)

SHINGLES thin pieces of wood overlapping in the manner of tiles, to form a roof covering.

SIMA gutter, often moulded in a distinctive form, from which derived the CYMA moulding.

SOFFIT exposed underside of an architectural element in, for instance, a CORNICE or ARCHITRAVE.

SPIRA concave moulding on the base of, for instance, a COLUMN. (See page 54.)

STOA extended PORTICO or roofed structure with a COLONNADE. (See page 162.)

STRING COURSE projecting horizontal course of structural elements or moulding.

STYLOBATE top step of a CREPIDOMA, forming the base for a COLONNADE. (See page 42.)

TENIA a FILLET running along the top of a DORIC ARCHITRAVE. (See page 42.)

TERRACOTTA baked clay (red in colour) used for construction or decoration of buildings or statues.

TETRASTYLE a PORTICO with four COLUMNS.

THOLOS dome, either freestanding or forming the centre of a circular building. (See pages 196, 199.)

TORUS large convex moulding, typically at the base of a COLUMN, of more or less semi-circular cross-section. (See page 54.)

TRABEATED structurally dependent on rectilinear POST and BEAM supports.

TRACHELION grooved moulding at the neck of a DORIC COLUMN, immediately below the ECHINUS. (See page 42.)

TRIGLYPH block carved with vertical channels, used between the METOPES in a DORIC FRIEZE. (See page 42.)

TUFA building stone of volcanic origin, more or less grey in colour.

TYMPANUM triangular area of a PEDIMENT enclosed by the CORNICES above and ENTABLATURE below; more generally, an area, usually recessed, formed by a LINTEL below and an arch above. (See page 42.)

VOLUTE scroll or spiral ornamental and/or support member, characteristic of IONIC CAPITALS. (See pages 52–53, 64–65.)

WATTLE AND DAUB method of making walls using thin twigs (wattles) interwoven and then plastered with mud or clay (daub).

bibliography

The books listed below are those the author found particularly useful as sources of general information on the architecture covered in this volume.

Bervé, H and Gruben, G, *Greek Temples, Theatres and Shrines*, New York 1962

Boardman, J, Griffin, J and Murray, O, *The Oxford History of the Classical World*, Oxford 1986

Carpenter, R, *The Architects of the Parthenon*, London 1970

Dinsmoor, W B, *The Architecture of Ancient Greece*, 3rd edition, London 1950

Lawrence, A W, *Greek Architecture*, London 1973

Levi, P, *Atlas of the Greek World*, Oxford 1980

Martienssen, R D, *The Idea of Space in Greek Architecture*, 2nd edition, Johannesburg 1964

Robertson, D S, *A Handbook of Greek and Roman Architecture*, 2nd edition, Cambridge 1943

Robertson, M, *A History of Greek Art*, Cambridge 1975

Sources of illustrations

pages 15, 61, 89, 103, 193, 197, 202 H Bervé and G Gruben, *Greek Temples, Theatres and Shrines*; pages 41, 53, 73, 79 W B Dinsmoor, *The Architecture of Ancient Greece*; pages 128, 142, 143 A W Lawrence, *Greek Architecture*; pages 46, 134, 166 D S Robertson, *A Handbook of Greek and Roman Architecture*; page 164 J B Ward-Perkins, *Cities of Ancient Greece and Italy*, London 1974

index

Figures in bold refer to the text; those in ordinary type refer to captions; and those in ordinary type with an asterisk refer to illustrations.